LIVES OF THEIR OWN

Studies in Rhetoric/Communication
Thomas W. Benson, Series Editor

LIVES OF THEIR OWN

*Rhetorical Dimensions in
Autobiographies of Women Activists*

Martha Watson

UNIVERSITY OF SOUTH CAROLINA PRESS

Published in Columbia, South Carolina, by the
University of South Carolina Press

Manufactured in the United States of America

03 02 01 00 99   5 4 3 2 1

Library of Congress Cataloging-in-Publication Data

Watson, Martha, 1941–
   Lives of their own : rhetorical dimensions in autobiographies of women
activists / Martha Watson, with James Kimble.
     p. cm. — (Studies in rhetoric/communication)
   Includes bibliographical references and index.
   ISBN 1-57003-200-9
   1. Autobiography—Women authors. 2. Biography as a literary form.
   3. Women social reformers—United States—Biography. I. Title. II. Series.
CT25.W28   1999
809'.93592072—dc21   97-45361

CONTENTS

Series Editor's Preface

In *Lives of Their Own,* Martha Watson, with James Kimble, examines as public rhetoric the autobiographies of women activists. In a sense all autobiography may be understood as rhetorical, in that it is by definition participating in a generic form and shaping the responses of its readers. Watson adds to these interests a focus on the ways women activists, and especially Emma Goldman, Frances Willard, Elizabeth Cady Stanton, Anna Howard Shaw, and Mary Church Terrell, constructed autobiographies as part of their lifework of public advocacy, argument, and agitation. She shows that these autobiographies attempted to advance the causes for which these women agitated—woman suffrage, temperance, racial and social justice. But rather than merely turning autobiography to public use, each of the autobiographers in her own way shows what it means to engage in a new mode of womanhood that redefines both the public and the private in light of each other.

Watson writes that, judged as public rhetoric, Emma Goldman's autobiography must be judged a failure—a failure that helps to illuminate the rhetoric of autobiography for today's readers, who are likely to be much more sympathetic to Goldman than were her contemporaries. Goldman's anarchism, argues Watson, which she presented as a rational necessity, seemed to her immediate audience to be in radical contradiction to her advocacy of a passionately liberated sexuality. Goldman's absolutism about anarchism and her individualism about sexual freedom, writes Watson, may have doomed the reception of the autobiography in its own day but may have helped to alter the very conventions that shaped the early reception of her work.

In contrast, James Kimble shows how Frances E. Willard, the leader of the Women's Christian Temperance Union and an active participant in other campaigns, re-created herself in her autobiography as having been inspired by God to devote herself, despite a feminine impulse to hesitancy and self-effacement, to progressive causes.

Watson demonstrates how Elizabeth Cady Stanton and Anna Howard Shaw take advantage of narrative and depictive rhetorics to describe the way they overcame obstacles they faced as women in living up to goals already accepted by society. She argues that though the result may have been fairly conservative, it was especially well adapted to its rhetorical moment and made good use of the power of autobiography to summon the power of direct experience.

Mary Church Terrell, an early African American feminist, lived with the burdens of both gender discrimination and racism. Martha Watson attributes the success of Church Terrell's autobiography to its deployment of what she describes as feminine rhetorical strategies—adopting a tone of modesty and defending her activism as an obligation for a woman who has been favored with opportunities and privileges. The rhetoric of Church Terrell, writes Watson, "provides a glimpse of the possibilities for her race if the force of racism can be constrained."

In their autobiographies the women who are studied in *Lives of Their Own* present themselves as public moral agents working against the constraints of social injustice. They become agents by struggling against adversity. However, their self-development is never merely personal—their actions are depicted as directed toward the benefit of others. Though the success of the public causes in which these women struggled was never more than partial, their autobiographical depictions of moral agency were themselves important rhetorical achievements.

Thomas W. Benson

PREFACE

This book, like many scholarly projects, has grown and changed as I have worked on it. Initially, with great innocence, I simply wished to explore autobiographies as a special form of public discourse. Although I have always had my professional home in a department of speech communication, I have had little interest in speeches, preferring instead to study other forms of discourse. My interest in autobiography grew directly out of my books on Emma Goldman and Anna Howard Shaw, both of whom wrote their life stories. These two women differed dramatically in their lives, their political allegiances, and the ways they wrote about themselves. Goldman's autobiography has enjoyed new popularity, chiefly among feminists who admire her assertiveness and sense of self. Shaw's work usually remains, deservedly I think, on a shelf gathering dust, of little interest to anyone but a scholar. Still, in their time, both works stemmed from a similar impulse: the desire of a person who had worked actively for a cause to demonstrate that her efforts and the cause she espoused were meaningful and important. In essence, I sensed that these works functioned in tandem with the speeches and writings of these women to urge public acceptance of, respectively, anarchism and woman suffrage. I became curious about the autobiographies of other persons who worked for social movements. My interest was not in the historical accuracy or psychological facets of these autobiographies. Rather, I was fascinated by how such narratives could argue and how their authors, successfully or not, could draw on the genre to advance their causes.

As I have worked on this book, I have often thought about how I would write my own life story. During the course of events I have had to compose two brief spiritual autobiographies, and the changes in those over the course of a few months have impressed me anew with how malleable our lives are. In telling to friends or to the public at large, we adapt our stories to the occasion, the audience, and our own needs.

Still, I know one theme will remain constant in my various tellings of my life: I have always benefited greatly from my friends and companions. This book emerged during a tumultuous period in my life, and a host of people, wittingly and unwittingly, helped me through that crisis and helped me with this work. My thanks first to Diane McGee, who struggled with me personally and professionally to bring this book to completion. The staff in the Dean's Office of the College of Arts and Humanities at the University of Maryland, College Park, were a source of constant encouragement and friendship: Judy

Abadia, Devonna Reddick, Linda Ringer, Diane West, and Joan Wood. My fellow associate deans were colleagues with whom I was privileged to work: Michele Eastman, Donna Hamilton, and Charles Rutherford. Robert Griffith, formerly dean of arts and humanities at Maryland and now provost at American University, had the courage to invite me, an outspoken faculty member, to join his staff; my time in his office has proved a wonderful experience, and I now, fortunately, count him among my friends. My thanks to all; the debt I owe you cannot be repaid.

My special scholarly thanks go to James Kimble, a Ph.D. candidate in the Department of Speech Communication at the University of Maryland. He was an extraordinary research assistant and helpful critic. He is solely responsible for the research and writing of chapter 4 of this book. In the writing of that chapter our roles largely reversed: I became his critic and guided his development of the argument, which was his own.

This book is dedicated with great love to Thing One and Thing Two, my daughters Karrin and Trenna, who have helped me write many of the happiest chapters in my life.

CHAPTER 1

AUTOBIOGRAPHIES AS PERSUASION

*A Rhetorical Perspective
on Personal Historical Narratives*

The women whose autobiographies make up the subject of this book were by any standard unusual individuals. That they managed to lead such active, successful, and productive lives in an era when women's roles were traditionally within the confines of the home is remarkable. They were not, of course, the first generation of women to forge a path into the mainstream of American public life. Nor were they the only women of their generation to be in the forefront of movements for social change. But, unlike most of their notable predecessors and cohorts, they published narratives of their own lives. This study of their autobiographies provides glimpses not only of the women themselves, but also of the genre as a dimension of public rhetorical discourse.

As many previous scholars have noted, women have traditionally written their lives differently from men both in form and in substance. Often uncomfortable with the assertiveness necessary to write an autobiography for publication, women have turned to diaries or other less public forms to record their life stories. So one notable fact about the autobiographies is that they exist at all. These women overcame the reticence often typical of their gender to write about their lives; the mere act of their writing distinguishes them from many of their predecessors and contemporaries. Some feminist critics have claimed that women do not so much record their lives as write themselves into existence. Seeking a distinctive feminist perspective on autobiography, Domna C. Stanton concluded:

> Although the injunction against writing had somewhat lifted for some women in contemporary places, autogynography, I thought, had a global and essential therapeutic purpose: to constitute the female subject. In a phallocentric system, which defines her as the object, the inessential other to the same male subject — that *The Second Self* had proved beyond a doubt — the *graphing* of the *auto* was an act of self-assertion that denied and reversed woman's status. It represented, as Didier had said of Sand's *My Life,* the conquest of identity through writing (p. 652). Creating the subject, an autograph gave the female "I" substance through the inscription of an interior and an anterior.[1]

Some of the women to be studied here had little apparent difficulty in asserting themselves as individuals. However, because of their role as leaders of social movements, in their autobiographies these women not only asserted themselves as women, they also articulated a model of selfhood for others to emulate. In writing their life stories, these women were expressing the possibility of a new kind of womanhood for others; in recording their life stories, these women were redefining womanhood and personhood for their contemporaries. To borrow and adapt Domna Stanton's terminology, they were constituting a new female subject.

Their roles as political activists and their reputations as exceptional women impacted their autobiographical acts in at least three ways: their construal of their reasons for writing, the place of their autobiographies in the corpus of their public discourse, and the attention they paid to their gender as a significant feature of their lives.

WRITING AN ACTIVIST WOMAN'S LIFE

These women wrote their autobiographies precisely because of the roles that they played in efforts for women's rights. The historian Gerda Lerner pinpoints this impulse quite explicitly, linking it to the development of a feminist consciousness: "The woman's rights and suffrage advocates were concerned with their place in History and showed it by writing each other's biographies, by writing their autobiographies, and by preserving their correspondence."[2] Thus, a consciousness of their roles rather than their individual desires prompted their autobiographies. At least by their admission, these women did not write their stories because they felt their lives as individuals worthy of particular notice. Rather, even the most assertive among them, Emma Goldman and Elizabeth Cady Stanton, traced their decisions to write autobiographies to pressures and encouragement from friends who insisted on the importance of their achievements. For example, Frances Willard's autobiography was "written by order of the National Woman's Christian Temperance Union." Mary Church Terrell warrants her writing to "a sense of justice and regard for truth" which impelled her to record her life. Displays of modesty are not restricted to women's autobiographies, and such ingratiating gestures are commonplace in public rhetoric. Regardless of the sincerity of her protestations that she was writing in response to pressure from others, each woman was keenly conscious of her role in and responsibility to a group advocating social change. She relates her life because of the importance of the cause she has advocated; for readers, her life story reflects the growth and strength of a movement.

In a related vein, each of these women dedicated a substantial portion of her adult life to working for social change: woman suffrage, temperance, racial and social justice. As speakers, writers, and leaders they argued and worked earnestly for their causes. Because of their highly visible public roles, their autobiographies became extensions of their public advocacy; their life stories complemented and supplemented their more explicitly agitative and argumentative discourses on behalf of their causes.

As they recall their lives, these authors, whether consciously or not, attest to readers about the importance, value, and significance of their causes and urge the readers' appreciation of their commitment. Their autobiographies also provide evidence of the impact of their ideology on their lives. Significantly, no matter what the intentions of these women in writing their life stories, their roles and their connections with particular causes color public perception of their autobiographies. Because the causes they espoused were controversial, their records of lives dedicated to these causes become part of the public discourse surrounding these topics.

Each autobiography reflects the importance of gender in the author's perception of her public role. The concern for "womanliness" that I see as integral to these works and that is a focus of the rhetorical analysis of the individual autobiographies suggests the complex pressures these women confronted in their public lives. Not only were they politically active and visible in an era when such publicness was somewhat unusual for women, but they worked for and supported causes to advance the rights of women. Elizabeth Cady Stanton, Anna Howard Shaw, Frances Willard, and Mary Church Terrell were all active in the woman suffrage movement as well as other controversial causes. Emma Goldman, the most prominent spokesperson for anarchism in her day, focused much of her rhetorical energy on advocating for the psychological, emotional, and physical liberation of women. (Interestingly, she did not support suffrage because it was part of a political system she deplored.) Thus, these women were in a difficult situation: as women, in their behaviors and activities they often defied social conventions, frequently in their efforts to gain still greater rights for women. But the success of their causes depends in part on the allegiance and support of other women, some of whom may be more timid about defying social mores. For their lives to be compelling as models for others and persuasive as evidence for their causes, these authors had to build identification with other women. Consequently, as they wrote their lives, they sought to affirm their womanliness in the face of charges that they had rejected the traditional feminine roles.

THE RHETORICAL CHALLENGES OF ACTIVIST AUTOBIOGRAPHIES

Any expository writing entails the common rhetorical tasks of selection, arrangement, effective presentation, and audience adaptation. Narrating one's life for an audience creates additional rhetorical challenges: one must select events from a lifetime and weave them into a coherent narrative; experiences that have no inherent meaning must be interpreted as part of a meaningful pattern. Barrett J. Mandel alludes to this autobiographical task: "Strictly speaking autobiography is not a recollection of one's life. Of course, everyone has recollections and memories. . . . They are spontaneous and natural. An autobiography, on the other hand, is an artifact, a construct from words."[3] An autobiography is, then, an at least partially fictionalized account of a life because looking back in retrospect the author imposes a meaning and coherence on events she did not possess at the moment they occurred. Thus, writing an autobiography entails the creation of a personal mythology. Georges Gusdorf concludes: "In the final analysis, then, the prerogative of autobiography consists in this: it shows us not the objective stages of a career—to discern these is the task of the historian—but that it reveals instead the effort of a creator to give meaning to his own mythic tale."[4] Moreover, this story as a whole must justify the telling; the author must demonstrate, either explicitly or implicitly, that her life has sufficient meaning and importance to warrant being recorded and being read.

Advocates for unpopular or controversial causes who use their autobiographies to reach supporters and potential followers must work to create life stories that will be both appealing and persuasive to readers. Readers of such an autobiography will be particularly interested in the reasons for the author's commitment to an ideal. Whether by depicting a sudden conversion experience, such as Saul on the road to Damascus, or a gradual coming to awareness growing out of vivid experiences, the author must offer a believable explanation of why she has adopted a particular outlook and ideology. Explicitly or implicitly, the autobiographer must explain her conversion in a compelling, or at least believable, way.

Most scholars agree that readers approach autobiographies with a desire to find some truth or guidelines for their own lives. In anticipation of this desire, ideally the social movement activist will depict a life that is imitable, one that supporters can emulate as they seek to advance the shared cause. But in narrating one's own life, especially if one has been in the forefront of an effort for social change, the temptation is to paint one's role as crucial, to minimize the failures while emphasizing the successes. The result may easily depict a larger-than-life person, a daring and courageous leader endowed with special gifts. Such a portrait, however, might daunt the would-be disciple. Thus, the tendency toward personal mythologizing that some scholars see as inherent to the genre may be in tension with the movement leader's propagandistic need to paint an imitable life.

For their part, readers will also test the author's experiences and reactions against their own. In writing, an autobiographer makes an implicit pact with the reader that she will tell truth as she perceives it about experiences and events. The reader peruses the work in search of truth, both about the author and the cause. Mandel observes:

The autobiography (as a genre) embodies truth when the reader seeks confirmation of his or her own perceptions of reality in terms of those experienced by another mortal. . . . Readers turn to autobiography to satisfy a need for verifying a fellow human being's experience of reality. They achieve satisfaction when they feel strongly that the book is true to the experience of the author and when they are aware, to a lesser degree, that the book is an achievement of literary construction, making use of pretense as a way of highlighting its opposite, reality.[5]

On the other hand, the movement leader approaches the task of writing her life story with a firm allegiance to a particular ideology. To write a compelling narrative, she must make her version of "truth" resonate with the reader. For their part, readers will test the story against reality as they know it and the ideology that has guided the life against their own perceptions. The skillful movement autobiographer must weave together the facts of history, the details of her own life, and the strands of her ideology with a sensitivity to the perhaps skeptical reader.

To this point, I have left the question of the readership for such autobiographies unexplored. Certainly, adherents and supporters will be drawn to read the life of the movement leader. They constitute the "given" audience, readers on whose sympathy the author can usually rely. But rhetorical discourse, as Maurice Charland has observed, has the power to *create* an audience.[6] According to Charland, Kenneth Burke's theory of identification assumes that "audience members . . . participate in the very discourse by which they would be 'persuaded.' Audiences would embody a discourse."[7] In essence, Charland argues that rhetorical narratives create an image of an agent, an individual capable of action. An audience member perceives the subject/agent projected in the discourse and may, if the rhetoric is effective, come to identify herself with it. He continues: "The process by which an audience member enters into a new subject position is therefore not one of persuasion. It is akin more to one of conversion that ultimately results in an act of recognition of the 'rightness' of a discourse and of one's identity with its reconfigured subject position."[8]

Charland's perspective suggests an additional rhetorical challenge for the authors whose works I study. As leaders of social movements and public advocates for their causes, they sought to attract supporters to assist in their efforts for social change. In writing their autobiographies, these women crafted an image of an activist for the causes they espoused; the image they project of themselves creates a "subject position," to borrow Charland's terminology, which they hope readers will choose to fill. In effect, these autobiographies function to *create* an audience for their causes; by offering an appealing image of womanhood through enactment in their own lives, they work to generate new support and allegiance among the formerly uncommitted.

5

These challenges, which confront a social activist in crafting her autobiography, provide a broad frame of reference for the analyses that will follow. Among the questions that guide my examination of particular texts are: How does each woman remain true to her distinctive experiences and qualities and yet create a life with which a diverse range of readers can identify? What of the possible tensions that may arise between autobiographers' desires to champion their causes and to write compelling narratives? How and how effectively do authors depict the reasons for their ideological commitments and justify their activism on their behalf? In their efforts to garner the support for women that is crucial to their causes, how do these women negotiate the boundaries of womanliness? Do they craft personae that would be attractive to established and potential followers? If so, how?

I first attempt to answer these questions by discussing the general rhetorical dimensions of historical writing, and then follow with more specific consideration of the approach I take in the case studies. Central to that approach is an understanding of narratives as a form of public moral argument and of the particular rhetorical resources autobiographies offer.

History as Rhetorical Narrative

The precise line between historical and fictional writing has long been a topic of lively discussion. However, as Lionel Gossman observes: "Although at times historical narrative and fictional narrative may seem to have been straining in opposite directions, they have both traditionally accepted the essential conditions of the classical narrative and have operated with the frame these provide."[9] Among those conditions that the two forms share, Gossman lists "the framing of the narrative, the establishment of a special time of narrative discontinuous with the time of the narrator's own telling," and the use of verb tenses that highlight the act of telling and establish a distinctive relation between author and reader.

If historical and literary works share the narrative form, the issue of the nature of the truth contained in each is problematic. Hayden White notes, "in general there has been a reluctance to consider historical narratives as what they most manifestly are—verbal fictions, the contents of which are as much invented as found and the forms of which have more in common with their counterparts in literature than they have with those in the sciences."[10] Louis O. Mink traces the "fictional" dimension in historical writing not to the manufacturing or deliberate distortion of facts as they are known, but to the historian's special need to perceive and argue for combinations of relationships among groups of facts.

The analysis and criticism of historical evidence can in principle resolve disputes about matters of fact or about the relations among facts, but not about the possible combinations of kinds of relations. The same event,

6

under the same description or different descriptions, may belong to different stories, and its particular significance will vary with its place in these different—often very different—narratives. . . . When it comes to the narrative treatment of an ensemble of interrelationships, we credit the imagination or the sensibility or the insight of the individual historian. . . . So narrative form in history, as in fiction, is an artifice, the product of the individual imagination. Yet at the same time it is accepted as claiming truth—that is, as representing a real ensemble of interrelationships in past actuality.[11]

While acknowledging the creative aspects of historical writing, Mink nonetheless insists on a critical difference between such narratives and "pure" fiction: "[F]or history both the structure of the narrative and its details are representations of past actuality: and the claim to be a true representation is understood by both writer and reader."[12]

This claim to truth gives historical writing potentially great persuasive force. Ronald Carpenter contends: "History can persuade. Discourse approached, read, and accepted by most people as historical writing embodies certain elements that allow it to shape attitudes and actions."[13] Because historical writing enjoys a presumption of credibility, Carpenter argues that it "acquires the status of being among the most persuasive discourse to influence attitudes and actions for the future." In particular, he notes that "people often read history for its lessons about life," hoping to find in the narrative guidelines for their own behaviors and beliefs.[14] Carpenter locates the persuasive potential of such writing in two broad features that are inherent in the process of composition: style and narrative. Carpenter, whose focus is on particular pieces of discourse by opinion leaders, seeks to explore what happens when the "inherently credible" medium of historical writing is coupled with the personal power of such individuals.

These observations about historical writing in general are, I believe, true of autobiography. Autobiography is a personal history, a retrospective on a life that tells one of many possible stories about the individual's experiences. And like other forms of history, its verisimilitude appeals to readers, who seek in it some "truth" about another human life. Also, as Carpenter indicates about other historical works, the author has two resources for achieving her persuasive ends: style and narrative.

However, autobiography differs from other history in one obvious and significant way: the author narrates her own life; she writes her own history. Most readers would readily grant that an individual is an "expert" on her life; thus, the narrator enjoys at least some of the credibility Carpenter sees as inherent for authors of history. Still, especially when the author is controversial or even notorious, being both narrator and subject of an allegedly historical work may erode some of the credibility enjoyed by opinion leaders.

Moreover, when the autobiography is a complement to the author's public discourse for a controversial issue or cause, the work becomes a venue for encouraging support and even activism from the reader.

The goal of this book is to explore how autobiographers who face these challenges, as well as the additional issue of gender, draw on the rhetorical resources of narrative to influence their readers. While I acknowledge the importance of style in persuasion, both the length of the works to be studied and the distinctive rhetorical challenges these women face place some limitations on this project. Style, despite its importance, will remain largely unexplored.

NARRATIVES AND THE LOGIC OF GOOD REASONS

Autobiographies argue, albeit differently from other forms of public discourse. Such a view forces consideration of how narratives can function as arguments and, if they are indeed arguments, how audiences can assess the claims implicit in them. Walter R. Fisher has explored precisely this question in some detail. Without fully rehearsing his explication and defense of narratives as a powerful — he would say primary — form of public moral argument, I would like to draw on his insights for my own discussion. While I agree with Fisher that narrative is the paradigm for public moral argument, that view need not be defended here. Autobiographies are, by any estimation, narratives, and what I wish to explore is the particular rhetorical functions of the autobiographical form.

In explicating the narrative paradigm, Fisher indicates that autobiography, along with history and biography, is a form of "recounting," the construction of a story to help ourselves and others "to establish a meaningful life-world. The character of the narrator(s), the conflicts, the resolutions, and the styles will vary, but each mode of recounting and accounting for is but a way of relating a 'truth' about the human condition."[15] As a form of public communication, narratives provide "good reasons" for actions and decisions because the narrator can explain the motivation and rationale behind her activities. As Fisher notes: "In theme, if not in every detail, narrative is meaningful for persons in particular and in general, across communities as well as cultures, across time and place. Narratives enable us to understand the actions of others because 'We all live out narratives in our lives and because we understand our own lives in terms of narratives.'"[16] Audiences are not, however, passive recipients of narratives, accepting their perspectives without question. Rather, they actively assess the stories they are told, questioning whether they do, indeed, provide "good reasons" for action.

In Fisher's view, audiences test narratives for probability (coherence) and fidelity. Testing of narrative probability occurs along three related axes: (1) the structural or argumentative coherence — does the "plot" of the story make sense; (2) material coherence—how does the story compare and contrast with other stories (that is, does it omit significant details); and (3) characterological coherence—are the central character's actions believable and reliable.[17] As audiences consider narratives, then, their first standard of judgment focuses on whether the story is coherent and convincing.

But coherence is only the first dimension of narrative rationality. Audiences also relate the narrative to their own lives to determine if the events and portrayals ring true to their own experiences. Fisher notes, "fidelity pertains to the individuated components of stories—whether they represent accurate assertions about social reality and thereby constitute good reasons for belief or action."[18] The issues of fact, relevance, consequence, consistency, and transcendency that Fisher sees as inherent in any logic of reasons are translated into a logic of "good reasons" that highlights the values implicit in the narrative. Briefly put, audiences sense the values implicit in a message and then question whether they are appropriate to the nature of the decision being advocated; what the consequences of adhering to those values are; whether the values in the message are confirmed and validated either in one's own life or in the lives of those one admires; and whether the values advocated constitute an ideal basis for human conduct[19] (108–9).

Fisher's arguments, as I have suggested, apply to the study of autobiographies. True, autobiographies differ from many narratives found in public discourse because they are a particular individual's recollections of events. For the most part, however, autobiographies proper are explicit narratives with a fairly clear chronological pattern.[20] These generic features of autobiographies—their chronological structure with a basis in real events and the status of the narrator as the central character—give them distinctive strengths and potentials as public moral argument from the perspective of Fisher's framework.

CHRONOLOGICAL STRUCTURE

The general chronological structure of autobiographies can serve as a significant rhetorical resource. Because the authors can unfold their lives and suggest the formative forces on their thinking, the reader can follow the course of their experiences. Knowing what the author has become, the reader can follow the author's development as a human being. For example, when we read of the childhood experiences of Elizabeth Cady Stanton in which her father repeatedly lamented that she was not a boy, we may sense the significance of those experiences on her later commitments. Cady Stanton's earnest efforts to overcome that barrier—to be like a boy—demonstrate clearly if obliquely for the reader the early sources of her zeal for women's rights. In a related vein, Frances Willard's artful reminiscing about her near idyllic childhood both convince readers of the importance of those experiences to her life and suggest the

9

validity of her lifelong commitment to "home protection." In essence, the chronological structure of autobiography allows the author to suggest indirectly but powerfully how she came to hold the convictions she cherishes.

A chronological narrative also encourages the author to recall anecdotes from her life and to relate vividly remembered experiences. The details of a life — colorful, poignant, embarrassing, humorous — can serve as evidence and examples to demonstrate the validity of the author's convictions. As an author relates a particular experience and weaves it into the pattern of her life, the reader receives concrete impressions both of the author's character and of her reasons for acting and believing as she does. Moreover, narratives can also provide vivid examples of the impact of the values the author espouses in her personal life. Emma Goldman's autobiography, for example, reveals both the perils and the joys of commitment to anarchism; Frances Willard can, under the guise of telling her story, indicate the praise, recognition, and support she has received in her work for temperance and women's rights. Narratives provide the authors the opportunity to enact the tenets of their ideologies and to demonstrate in their lives the beneficent impact of their causes.

Telling a life chronologically can also permit authors to frame particular events in ways that shape the reader's interpretation of them. In most of the works I examine, the authors, whether intentionally or not, with attention to issues of home, family, and womanliness, establish a network of values with which most of their readers could identify. For example, Willard rhapsodizes about her happy childhood home; Cady Stanton appropriately tells of her childhood, marriage, and family life before discussing her involvement with women's rights. Strategically, the chronological structure permits the authors to establish common ground with their readers, to build a bond with them before discussing more controversial and potentially divisive topics.

The typical chronological structure of autobiographies can become significant in highlighting shared values. Appropriately beginning their stories in childhood, authors can gradually lead their readers to the saga of their public lives. In effect, the personal frames the public; the reader first gets to know the author as a private person whose early experiences and reminiscences can craft a humanly appealing persona. Even the reader who is fully aware of the author's public activities gets to know another side of the personality, one that may disarm criticism as it charms.

THE AUTHOR'S VOICE

The act of writing an autobiography signals an author's willingness to share her life with others. On the other hand, readers approach autobiographies with a desire to learn something of another's experiences. This autobiographical pact provides an important rhetorical resource for the author in several respects.

Sharing one's life with another establishes a certain level of intimacy and connection between the author and her reader. The author can freely discuss topics that might be inappropriate in a public speech; these need not be about intimate matters. For example, Emma Goldman reveals how impressed she was by a vase of roses in the office of her employer; her memory of this is poignant because she realized that as a worker she herself could not afford a single blossom. This small detail, insignificant in itself, provides a glimpse of Goldman's aesthetic side. Simultaneously of course, it highlights the inequities that her ideology sought to correct. But the attentive reader develops some sense of "knowing" Goldman in a way not always possible from speeches or other written documents.

At the same time, the author's voice carries unusual weight in an autobiography. Simply put, the author tells her side of the story. Certainly, the reader can and will (if Fisher's notion of fidelity is accurate) test some of the details against her or his own experience. But the author is free and, indeed, is fully expected to explain her perceptions and her interpretations of events. We may question whether we would respond as the author did to a particular situation or we may disagree with some of her actions. Nonetheless, we cannot deny that she is the authority on her own life. And if the author has won our confidence with appealing stories of her childhood or poignant recollections of her disappointments, we as readers are predisposed to attend to her voice, to try at least to understand her behaviors and decisions.

BUILDING COMMON GROUND: RHETORIC AS IDENTIFICATION

The two significant resources of autobiographical narratives that I have explored, the chronological structure and the authorial voice, in tandem work to build a bridge between the authors and their readers. Because of their abiding commitment to social change, these women's lives were embedded in controversy. Each of them chose to advocate change; in so doing, they placed themselves in opposition to many potential readers; their views about controversial issues often clashed with their readers'. To be persuasive, then, authors had to draw readers to themselves, to overcome objections and hesitancies as they told their stories. The rhetorical theorist Kenneth Burke sees this process of building identification as the key to persuasion and argues that "identification" rather than "persuasion" is the key term in rhetoric.

To begin, Burke notes that rhetoric, however construed, is *rooted in an essential function of language itself, . . . the use of language as a symbolic means of inducing cooperation in beings that by nature respond to symbols.*"[21] Inducing cooperation, in turn, depends on the rhetor leading the reader or listener to "identify" or be "consubstantial" with her. In other words, we persuade others by establishing common ground with them. Such common ground may include shared experiences, background, origin, interests, or attitudes as well as other things. The significant fact is that the listener or reader realizes that she or he shares certain features with the rhetor; those shared features become the basis for cooperation. Burke observes:

> You persuade a man only insofar as you can talk his language by speech, gesture, tonality, order, image, attitude, idea, *identifying* your ways with his. Persuasion by flattery is but a special case of persuasion in general. But flattery can safely serve as our paradigm if we systematically widen its meaning, to see behind it the conditions of identification or consubstantiality in general. And you give the "signs" of such consubstantiality by deference to an audience's "opinions." For the orator, following Aristotle and Cicero, will seek to display the appropriate "signs" of character to earn the audience's good will. True, the rhetorician may have to change an audience's opinion in one respect; but he can succeed only insofar as he yields to the audience's opinions in other respects. Some of their opinions are needed to support the fulcrum by which he would move other opinions.[22]

The concept of "identification" as outlined by Burke provides an excellent vantage point for considering autobiographies as rhetorical narratives. A primary challenge faced by the women activists whose works are studied is building identification with their readers in order to influence their attitudes toward the controversial issues advocated. The focus of this analysis is exploring how these authors craft their narratives to build identification, particularly in depicting the sources of their commitments to causes and their impact on their lives.

Burke provides additional help in explicating the bases of identification. The key to his perspective is the pentad, the five terms that will emerge in any human discussion of motives. Burke observes: "In any rounded statement about motives you must have some word that names the *act* (names what took place, in thought or deed), and another that names the *scene* (the background of the act, the situation in which it occurred); also, you must indicate what person or kind of person (*agent*) performed the act, what means or instruments he used (*agency*), and the *purpose*."[23] A critic can scrutinize discourse to determine both how the rhetor names each of these elements and which she emphasizes in her depiction. The naming and the emphasis will indicate the bases on which the rhetor encourages identification with her audience.

This method, which Burke labels *dramatism,* departs significantly from traditional approaches to rhetoric. Most earlier theorists view rhetoric as argumentative or demonstrative; that is, rhetors construct arguments, inductive or deductive, to persuade listeners about the truth or validity of their positions. While Burke would not deny that rhetorical discourse often uses an argumentative structure, a dramatistic analysis will reveal the depiction underlying such arguments.

Burke's view of rhetoric and his dramatistic method undergird the perspective I employ in these case studies. While I do not use the pentad explicitly to structure the case studies in part 2, I return to it in discussing the autobiographies in general in the final chapter. The narrativity implicit in Burke's system informs my study of the autobiographies individually. In essence, the pentad and Burke's dramatism view rhetorical discourse as primarily narrative rather than demonstrative. Not only do I find this view of rhetoric compelling, but also a narrative approach to rhetoric is particularly appropriate for studying explicitly narrative works such as autobiography.

The case studies that comprise the majority of this book explore these autobiographies as rhetorical narratives that work to build identification between author and reader. As they affirm a cause, offer a model, and record a life, they seek to garner support and defend commitment to a cause. This chapter has provided the rhetorical underpinnings of this work. Chapter 2 explores the attempts to define autobiography as a genre and reviews with quite broad strokes previous scholarship in this area. It provides the definition of autobiography that guides this book as well as suggesting how the focus of this work differs from earlier research.

Section 2 of the book consists of four case studies, each of which focuses on one or more of the questions mentioned earlier. The chapter on Emma Goldman, which begins the second section of the book, explores her depiction of her conversion. The central argument of that chapter is that Goldman's narration of her conversion, a crucial event for a social movement autobiography, provides an unpersuasive and ineffective explanation of that crucial event. The following chapter on Frances Willard suggests how she shrewdly and convincingly explains both her commitment and her controversial actions by warranting her behavior in the process of Christian revelation, an appeal well suited to her audience. Thus, in tandem these chapters suggest some of the pitfalls and potentials of autobiography as a persuasive tool, particularly in the realm of explaining conversion and commitment.

The chapter that examines the autobiographies of Elizabeth Cady Stanton and Anna Howard Shaw demonstrates several effective strategies these women employ in explaining their commitment to woman's rights and in modeling the new woman they hope their followers will become. One thesis of this chapter is that these women draw on the resources and potential of autobiography to provide a compelling argument about women's rights as well as an attractive model of a new woman. In their writing they constitute a new female subject for their readers to contemplate and emulate.

The final case study, of Mary Church Terrell, highlights how she used her own exceptional life to answer allegations about the supposed inferiority of her race; to suggest how other African American women could lead useful, meaningful lives despite widespread racism; and to affirm possibilities for racial harmony and justice. Like Cady Stanton and Shaw, she offered a new image of woman, one constrained by race but triumphant over both racial and gender stereotypes.

Chapter 7 attempts to consider these works together and to explore how they argue. Returning to the ideas of Kenneth Burke mentioned in this first chapter, chapter 7 contends that these books share a common rhetorical pattern, an emphasis on scene as propelling an agent to commitment for a purpose. This pattern has rhetorical advantages that I discuss briefly. In addition, this chapter returns to the theme expressed by Domna Stanton about women's writing as constituting a feminine self and argues that these works opened a rhetorical space for women to discuss and revise their notions of their womanhood.

Taken together, the case studies explore how these autobiographers craft arguments that speak to the authors' reasons for commitment to causes, the influence of those causes on their lives, and the truth of their ideology. Because all of these women sought to extend the rights of women and to alter social constraints on their behavior, in their lives they also provided a new model of womanhood and womanly behavior. One goal of this work is to demonstrate that autobiography as a genre offers movement leaders an array of rhetorical resources that they can draw on to argue for their causes as they record their lives. The chronological flow of the narrative, which includes the concrete incidents of a life and the image of the individual that emerges in a sustained story told by the author, creates a distinctive bond between author and reader that can have tremendous persuasive impact. These case studies explore how these women draw on these resources, effectively or ineffectively, to make their lives and their causes compelling to their readers.

CHAPTER 2

THE NATURE OF AUTOBIOGRAPHY

To a contemporary American, the notion of autobiography is commonplace. Indeed, writing about one's life or a portion of it is often a schoolroom exercise. Albert E. Stone notes, "autobiography is firmly rooted in our culture—and . . . not simply in high literary culture."[1] Although the term *autobiography* was not coined until 1797, self-told life stories in the form of memoirs and reminiscences as well as diaries have been available for centuries.[2] In this country, the writing of autobiography has flourished since the end of the eighteenth century.[3] Today the proliferation of autobiographies in bookstores attests to Americans' predilection for and fascination with the form. Any notion that autobiographies are innocent reflections on the course of one's life, perhaps with an eye to sharing lessons learned, is belied by modern publishing practices. Contemporary readers have become inured to the appearance of autobiographies by celebrities still in robust health and often far from old.

DEBATING THE GENRE

Although most readers have little difficulty recognizing an autobiography, scholars have found the form complex and elusive, seemingly incapable of precise definition. Perhaps the only agreement about autobiography as a genre among theorists is the "I-ness" of its subject. Georges Gusdorf, in his seminal essay on autobiography, contends that "the conscious awareness of the singularity of each individual life is the late product of a specific civilization."[4] Citing Augustine's *Confessions* as "a brilliantly successful landmark at the beginning" of this distinctive period, Gusdorf insists that autobiography as a genre expresses a concern peculiar to Western culture: the belief that an individual life can be "worthy of a special interest."[5] His sweeping generalization about the distinctive "westernness" of the autobiographical impulse is as difficult to refute as to prove; still, some sense of one's self as significant is necessary to undertake the crafting of an autobiography. At this point the distinction between autobiographies and related forms such as diaries is crucial. The conscious decision to write one's life story for publication—the decision to write "an autobiography"—is rooted not only in the author's awareness of her individuality but also in her belief that her life is either significant or meaningful.[6]

Despite its popularity as a genre, autobiography defies easy definition and categorization. Sidonie Smith notes, "This genre, apparently so simple, so self-evident, so readily accessible to the reader, is ultimately as complex as the subject it seeks to capture in its representation and as various as the rhetorical expressions through which, with the mediation of language, that subjectivity reads itself into the world."[7] Perhaps hyperbolically, James Olney notes, "autobiography is not so much a mode of literature as literature is a mode of autobiography—and not by any means the only possible mode."[8] Central issues in scholarly discussions of autobiography are its status and integrity as a genre. The difficulties of distinguishing the autobiography from other similar works (memoirs, diaries, reminiscences) and from its fictional counterpart, the autobiographical novel, have perplexed scholars. Also, the variety of forms that autobiographies can assume—from poetry to prose narrative to novels—further clouds its generic status. As Olney observes, "everyone knows what autobiography is, but no two observers, no matter how assured they may be, are in agreement."[9] Because of the disparate forms and features of autobiographical works, some scholars despair of defining the genre on those bases. For example, Paul Jay resists the idea that even purely self-reflexive narratives can be classified as autobiography "in any coherent or helpful way."[10] Citing James Olney's admission that there may be "no way to bring autobiography to heel as a literary genre with its own proper form, terminology, and observances," Jay insists, "there will always be the temptation in defining autobiography as a genre either to create borders that are too exclusively narrow or ones that are so large as to be meaningless."[11]

To demonstrate the difficulties, Jay delineates the problems that emerge when one tries to indicate whether a particular text is, in fact, an autobiography. Citing Wordsworth's *The Prelude* and *The Autobiography of Benjamin Franklin,* Jay notes that their status as autobiographies is a difference in degree, not kind, since both are self-reflections on the author's life and both are literary constructions.[12] On the other hand, treating such diverse works as a single, unified genre is also problematic because some clearly autobiographical works (*The Education of Henry Adams*) often violate usual characteristics of the genre (narration in the first person), while other works, such as Wordsworth's *Prelude* (widely regarded as autobiographical), fit equally well into other genres (the epic in this case).

Jay's solution is to abandon the attempt to define the genre by reference to textual features—such as the use of first person in the narrative or its prose rather than poetic form. Instead, he proposes that the defining feature of the genre is that each autobiography is a response to a distinctive literary exigency: "its author's confrontation with a particular problem—the problem of literary self-representation."[13] Rather than defining autobiographies textually, Jay locates them as a response to a particular literary challenge. The form, substance, and style of that response may differ radically.[14]

ESTABLISHING THE PARAMETERS

Other scholars, however, have attempted quite rigorous definitions. Among these, Roy Pascal and Phillipe LeJeune have paid particular attention to defining the form rather precisely and rather narrowly. While acknowledging the confusion and uncertainty that surround the term, Pascal argues the necessity of distinguishing "autobiography proper and other literary forms that have an autobiographical content."[15] Pascal's perception of that necessity stems from his central concern, which is the nature of truth in autobiography. Quite readily Pascal admits that all writing may be autobiographical in some sense; but he is most concerned with distinguishing the autobiography from other expository prose forms. In his view autobiography, though similar to such forms as diaries and reminiscences, "involves a distinctive attitude on the part of the author, a distinctive mode of presentation.[16] Unlike a diary, which "moves through a series of moments of time," an autobiography "is a review of a life from a particular moment"; unlike memoirs or reminiscences, in which the attention may be focused on others, in the autobiography the author's attention is on the self to a degree that would seem vain in other forms.[17] However, the focus is on the self in the world, struggling with and against forces to achieve some sense of identity and wholeness. Having drawn these distinctions, Pascal offers his own definition of an autobiography, worth quoting at length here because it reflects part of the perspective I will adopt in this book.

> These distinctions have led us a good way towards a definition of autobiography proper. It involves the reconstruction of the movement of a life, or a part of a life, in the actual circumstances in which it was lived. Its centre of interest is the self, not the outside world, though necessarily the outside world must appear so that, in give and take with it, the personality finds its peculiar shape. But "reconstruction of a life" is an impossible task. A single day's experience is limitless in its radiation backward and forward. So that we have to hurry to qualify the above assertions by adding that autobiography is a shaping of the past. It imposes a pattern on a life, constructs out of it a coherent story. It establishes certain stages in an individual life, makes links between them, and defines, implicitly or explicitly, a certain consistency of relationship between the self and the outside world. . . . This coherence implies that the writer takes a particular standpoint, the standpoint of the moment at which he reviews his life, and interprets his life from it. The standpoint may be the actual social position of the writer, his acknowledged achievement in any field, his present philosophy; in every case it is his present position which enables him to see his life as something of a unity, something that may be reduced to order. Autobiography, as A. M. Clark said, is not the annals of a man's life, but its "philosophical history. . . . Autobiography is then an interplay, a collusion, between past

and present; its significance is indeed more the revelation of the present situation than the uncovering of the past."[18]

Pascal believes that readers demand "more than an account of personalities, events, and circumstances" when they read autobiographies. "These must become the framework, in some sense the embodiment, of the personality of the writer as a man pledged to life."[19] Because readers seek this sense of a real person in the autobiography, Pascal declines to broaden his definition to include autobiographical novels, although he admits how much they can tell about the author.

Philippe LeJeune, who takes great pains to explicate the textual characteristics of the form, provides a concise definition of the genre close in spirit to that of Pascal: "Definition: Retrospective prose narrative written by a real person concerning his own existence, where the focus is his individual life, in particular the story of his personality."[20] Like Pascal, LeJeune admits that a variety of forms—memoirs, biography, personal novel, autobiographical poem, journal/diary, self-portrait, or essay—may satisfy *some* of these requirements; but only the true autobiography and the autobiographical novel can satisfy all of them.[21]

In his early work LeJeune averred that no *internal* textual evidence distinguished those two forms; only the *external* evidence of the author's intentionality could differentiate between them.[22] Later, however, LeJeune modified his position to argue that an "autobiographical pact" between author and reader makes a clear distinction possible. The autobiographical pact is an agreement between author and reader about the nature of the work. Such a pact can be established either *explicitly* (the name of the narrator-protagonist is given in the narrative and is the same as that of the author) or *implicitly* (a title such as *The Autobiography of,* which signals the intention of the work or an initial section of the text in which the author signals s/he is also the protagonist).[23] This "autobiographical pact" between author and reader "determines the mode of reading of the text and engenders the effects which, attributed to the text, seem to thus define it as autobiography."[24] As Barrett J. Mandel writes, autobiography achieves its status as autobiography from the reader's involvement with it: "The point is that fiction is fiction *for a subject*. Autobiography is autobiography *for a subject*."[25] Thus, the general agreement and cooperation of both author and reader are necessary to make a work an autobiography.

But for the type of autobiographies I wish to examine, those written by leaders of social movements, the autobiographical pact between reader and author provides more than a useful distinguishing characteristic of the genre. The reader's intention in perusing the book, her or his interest in the life as well as cause of the author, and receptiveness to the lessons gleaned from the work create a form of interpersonal communication between the author and reader. Jean Starobinski alludes to the communicative link between reader and author:

> Autobiography is certainly not a genre with rigorous rules. It only requires that certain possible conditions be realized, conditions that are mainly ideological (or cultural): that the personal experience be important, that it offer an opportunity for a sincere relation with someone else. These presuppositions establish the legitimacy of "I" and authorize the subject of the discourse to take his own past existence as theme. Moreover, the "I" is confirmed in the function of permanent subject by the presence of the correlative "you," giving clear motivation to the discourse.[26]

Every autobiographer writes to and for an audience; every audience member reads the book to learn more about the author. Because autobiographies usually contain at least some details of the author's personal life, the work establishes a greater degree of intimacy between the reader and the writer. But in the case of narratives by social movement leaders, both author and reader share an additional interest: the cause to which the author has devoted her life. Within such works the author must at least suggest to the sympathetic reader the reasons for her commitment to a cause and the impact of it on her life. Thus, each of these autobiographies is a form, albeit an attenuated one, of interpersonal communication in which the author speaks about the motivations for her commitment to a receptive, if perhaps doubtful, reader. This interpersonal linkage adds to these works' force as public rhetorical documents.

AUTOBIOGRAPHIES IN THE SOCIAL CONTEXT

Despite my general acceptance of their views, I believe that the approach of Pascal and LeJeune tends to obscure the impact of social mores and practices on the form, substance, and style that one adopts in writing a life story. Women's writing of their life stories demonstrates this limitation clearly.[27]

As Patricia Meyer Spacks observes, women have faced different obstacles than men in writing their life stories and have often, as a consequence, recorded their lives without recourse to the "proper" autobiography.

> Commitment to formal autobiography, a story of the self written with the intent of dissemination, implies also a claim of significance—a fact that troubled early [women] practitioners, who felt obliged to defend themselves against the charge of vanity by asserting the exemplary shape of their experience or the didactic intent of their prose. Women, for obvious social reasons, have traditionally had more difficulty than

men about making public claims of their own importance. They have excelled in the writing of diaries and journals, which require no such claims, more than in the production of total works offering a coherent interpretation of their lives.[28]

In her study of the autobiographies of women who were active in the public realm in the nineteenth century, Spacks argues that the language, the tone, and the details of their narratives as well as their form reflect a tension between their public and private roles not found in the works of men.[29]

Gender may also have a clear impact on substance. Estelle C. Jelinek notes in the preface to her book on women's autobiographies that women tend to write about "remarkably similar" subjects and "the emphasis remains on personal matters—not the professional, philosophical, or historical events that are more often the subject of men's autobiographies."[30] Thus, even when they adopt the same form as men do in writing their life stories, women may tell their tales differently. For example, women, who have traditionally been discouraged from viewing themselves as public agents, may focus their autobiographies less on their individual lives than on their lives as lived for others.

On a different level, Sidonie Smith takes issue with all "normative" definitions of autobiography and any attempt to judge such works in relation to public life and discourse. She writes:

> Patriarchal notions of woman's inherent nature and consequent social roles have denied or severely proscribed her access to the public space; and male distrust and consequent repression of female speech have either condemned her to public silence or profoundly contaminated her relationship to the pen as an instrument of power. If she presumes to claim a fully human identity by seeking a place in the public arena, therefore, she transgresses patriarchal definitions of female nature by enacting the scenario of male selfhood. As she does so, she challenges the cultural conceptions of the nature of woman and thereby invites public censure for her efforts. If she bows to the discursive pressure for anonymity, however, she denies her desire for a voice of her own.[31]

Moreover, Smith objects to imposing the standard of "representativeness" in assessing women's autobiographies. Because women have traditionally been discouraged from participating in the public realm, those who have done so have been seen as "exceptional" or aberrant rather than representative. In some cases, then, female autobiographers, to build identification with their readers, may need to overcome the charge that they are highly unusual or even "manly." On the other hand, women who have recorded their lives during such repressed periods may create life stories that are more typical of the male than of the female of the era.[32]

In this project these issues become especially salient since I consider the autobiographies of women who were committed to active advocacy for social changes that would affect their own status and roles. Moreover, the period on which this work focuses, the late nineteenth and early twentieth centuries, was a period of great flux in social definitions of gender roles for both men and women.[33] For women, in particular, the period marked a transition from Victorian notions of "True Womanhood," which consigned middle-class women to the domestic sphere and sharply delineated "appropriate" female behaviors, to a new model of womanhood, which offered females greater latitude in their behaviors. Thus, the women who wrote the works I examine had to address not only the issues surrounding the causes to which they were committed, but also their roles as women. To reach a broad audience for their causes, they had to negotiate the treacherous waters of what constituted acceptable and even admirable female behavior. As a consequence, their autobiographies reflect, however subtly, the social tensions surrounding the notion of womanhood.[34]

Although objections to the approaches of Pascal and LeJeune are not limited to their neglect of the constraining function of social norms on women and other groups, this short discussion reflects issues that must be addressed in the consideration of individual autobiographies. These same arguments apply to other marginalized groups. Thus, the case studies, which comprise the second portion of this book, draw attention to how social forces and practices influenced the writing of the autobiographies I study. My goal is to be sensitive to the distinct rhetorical obstacles persons confront in writing their life stories and to describe the particular strategies they use to overcome these.

THE CRITICISM OF AUTOBIOGRAPHY

The struggle over the definition of autobiography has not discouraged the study of the form. Indeed, the critical scholarship on autobiographies is both so abundant and so varied that summarizing it is difficult. But I must explore the range of work, albeit somewhat superficially, to distinguish the focus of the present project and to suggest how my approach both builds on and extends previous scholarship.

In her introduction to *A Poetics of Women's Autobiography,* Sidonie Smith offers a convenient, although admittedly oversimplified, history of research on autobiography based on earlier surveys by William C. Spengemann and James Olney. She perceives three distinct phases of work on autobiography, focusing on facticity, psychology, and textuality. In the first phase, stretching from the late nineteenth to the early twentieth century, scholars were concerned with the *bios* of the autobiographer and were especially interested in the "truth" contained in such works. Such critics "evaluated the quality of life as it was lived and the veracity of the autobiographer as he or she narrated the story of that life."[35] The concern of these critics was, then, historical accuracy. The autobiographer's role and involvement in telling her story were unproblematic. Olney notes that the naive assumptions were that an author could "narrate his life in a manner at least approaching an objective historical account . . . that there was nothing problematic about the *autos*, no agonizing questions of identity, self-definition, self-existence, or self-deception."[36] Such criticism examines autobiographies as historical discourse, assessing the material in the works as more or less accurate reflections of experiences and events.

To the next generation of critics, however, the *auto* was all-important. They attended:

> to the "agonizing" questions inherent in self-representation. For these critics, truthfulness becomes a much more complex and problematic phenomenon. Since autobiography is understood to be a process through which the autobiographer struggles to shape an "identity" out of amorphous subjectivity, the critic became a psychoanalyst of sorts, interpreting the truth of an autobiography in its psychological dimensions rather than in its factual or moral ones. . . . The autobiographical act is conceived as creative or interpretative.[37]

This approach highlights autobiographies as artistically crafted rather than simply historically narrated stories. Questions of the author's motivation and the social forces that shape how she tells her story become the focus of attention.

In the next period critics challenged the notion of referentiality in autobiographies by questioning the "comfortable assumptions about an informing 'I.'"[38] Such critics argue that the *autos*, shattered by the influence of the unconscious and controlled by linguistic conventions, "may be nothing more, and certainly nothing less, than a convention of time and space where symbolic systems, existing as infinite yet always structured possibility, speak themselves in the utterance of a *parole*."[39] In short, the *autos* in autobiography does not exist except within the words of the text.[40] Other modern critics emphasize the acts of reading that constitute the autobiographical exchange.

Each phase of criticism has enriched my understanding of particular texts as well as the genre. But each has different implications for my project. Moreover, it is important to note both that the approaches are not always distinct and that work in each of these veins continues today. The first vein, which focuses on the facticity of an individual autobiography, is the least significant for the present project. For the present purposes the relationship between a work and historical factuality is salient only to the extent that the reader may assess the narrative's truthfulness as part of her response to her work. To borrow Walter R. Fisher's language, I will be concerned with how the reader tests the narrative's coherence and fidelity to determine if it constitutes sound moral argument.[41] The vein of criticism, which examines how the reader constructs her narrative, raises questions of strategic adaptation (particularly in building ethos through the creation of persona) that are central to the rhetorical perspective I will adopt. The final phase, which examines the nature of meaning in an autobiography and how readers construct their own interpretations of the text, is germane to my consideration of works as forms of public argument. For these reasons, I will limit my attention to the critical works that focus on questions of psychology and textuality—the last phases in Smith's schema—to develop the groundwork for my project.

THE QUESTION OF SELF-REPRESENTATION

Intention and Motive as Decision

Concerned with each author's self-representation, these critics searched for recurrent patterns to establish subgenres or types and documented the strategies authors employed in works; they also considered the forces that have shaped autobiographies into different forms. This vein of scholarship has been extremely productive but has yielded little firm agreement. Two broad concerns have dominated this scholarship: (1) the intention or motive of the author in writing the work—what she seeks to do in the work; and (2) the forces that have influenced the evolution of the genre by shaping the author's mode of re-creating her life story. At times, these foci interpenetrate. For the group of critics who consider what the author intends to do or is doing in her autobiography issues of intention, crafting of a persona, and thematic development emerge.

In an early study Arthur Melville Clark argues that the literal "truth" of an autobiography is far less important than the "higher artistic truth in the total impression left. . . . If the reading of an autobiography is a good substitute for the author's presence and conversation, it is a good autobiography though its author was a liar of the first magnitude."[42] Recognizing that an autobiography is a mixture of truth and fiction, Clark sees the form and substance of a work as emerging from the author's motivation in writing. From his perspective,

> every autobiographer . . . has passed through a kind of crisis short and intense or protracted and cumulative in its effects affecting mind, body, or estate, private or shared with others. . . . This experience is, in biological terms, the releasing stimulus. It has somehow isolated him from his fellows and produced a degree of loneliness, a kind of need, more insistent than his normal mistrust of his fellows, for either sympathy or self-justification, or appreciation, or communication.[43]

These motivations, which shape the writing and determine the theme of the work, form the basis for Clark's generic categories. An autobiography may reflect the author's desire to appeal for sympathy, her need to justify herself, her effort to garner appreciation, or her impulse to express herself creatively.[44] Thus, from Clark's perspective, the most significant force in shaping the form of the autobiography is the author's rhetorical purpose and stance.[45]

Pursuing a similar vein, William L. Howarth explores what an author attempts to *do* in narrating his/her life. To determine this, he works from a simple analogy: "an *autobiography* is a *self-portrait*."[46] In writing his life story the autobiographer "artfully defines, restricts, or shapes that life into a self-portrait—one far different from his original model, resembling life but actually composed and framed as an artful invention."[47] Despite their disparities, Howarth contends that all autobiographies have three key elements that reflect the strategies open to their authors: the depiction of character, the techniques used within the work (style, imagery, structure), and the broad themes developed.[48] He identifies three subgenres of autobiography, each of which reflects a particular stance on the part of the author; that stance, in turn, determines how the author will handle the three common elements.

In the oratorical autobiography the author assumes the persona of a messiah who preaches an ideology. Typically using the techniques of parallelism, refrain, and amplification, the author takes vocation as her theme because she seeks to represent in her life "an idealized pattern of human behavior."[49] (88–89). In the autobiographies that Howarth identifies as dramas, the author is an actor, performing a series of roles. Offering no thesis about his development and preaching no sermon, the author "vividly impersonates, or dramatizes, several irreverent notions."[50] With a focus on idiosyncracies, the author plays to his audience, sometimes shamelessly. The final form, autobiography as poetry, is an exercise in continuing self-study.[51] "Poetic autobiographers can also draw only tentative, experimental self-portraits. They share equally strong doubts, especially about their current state of mind. Uncertain of the present, they study the past for some explanation of their later difficulties."[52] Their theme is development; their techniques, lyrical and poetic description. Thus, Howarth's categories reflect the rhetorical stance and goals of the author, as do Clark's, albeit from a different angle of vision.

Pascal's concern with the nature of truth in autobiographies determines his categorization of the subgenres. Contending that "to give the truth about oneself has always been the aim of true autobiography," Pascal nevertheless admits how difficult that goal is to attain. Errors of fact creep in through lapses of memory and because of scruples about revealing information about others. In addition, structure and style may impede the author in her search for truth telling. According to Pascal, truth will not be objective in autobiographies, but rather can only be determined in regard to the authors' general intentions. Thus, he divides the genre into four broad groups based on "the specific personality and intention of the author, as a scientist, a statesman, a poet, and so on."[53] He then explores the nature of truth in the autobiographies of poets and writers of imaginative literature, those dedicated to a particular philosophy, those called to a particular vocation, and those persons whose focus is on their childhood. He categorizes autobiographies according to how the authors interpret the larger meaning they perceive in their lives; he studies their "truthfulness" not in comparison to some absolute standard but instead in relation to how fully the author is able to communicate the intuitive truth she has perceived.

Also concerned with the author's perceptions about her own life, Olney distinguishes autobiographies on the basis of how self-aware and self-reflexive the author appears to be. In the autobiography simplex the author does little self-reflection. She may depict a life devoted to a particular cause or ideology without reflecting on the source of her commitment or providing a rationale for choosing a particular ideology. These books are filled with activities and events, with little struggling on the authors' part about how to interpret or react to the pace of life. In contrast, in the autobiography duplex the author reveals her wrestling with different interpretations of life and disparate ideologies.[54] Through these works the authors share with the reader their private struggles and doubts, the processes through and by which they arrived at the point in life at which their books were written.

EXTERNAL FORCES AS FORMATIVE

Another group of scholars has explored the factors that have shaped the writing of such works at particular times. Since these critics draw attention to how context and situation shape autobiographical texts, the difference in focus between them and the two groups is often a matter of degree. The works of Karl J. Weintraub and William Spengemann reflect the linkage between context and content. Weintraub contends that autobiographical writings from Saint Augustine up to Goethe reveal "a gradual emergence of [a sense of] individuality" that was largely missing in classical society.[55] Consequently, social, literary, and historical forces have influenced the forms, themes, and substance of works. Acknowledging the difficulties of definition, Spengemann argues that the student of autobiography must view it historically, "not as the one thing that writers have done again and again, but as the pattern described by the various things they have done in response to changing ideas about the nature of the self, the ways in which the self may be apprehended, and the proper methods of reporting those apprehensions."[56] Accordingly, his analysis traces "the evolution of autobiographical forms," beginning with *The Confessions of St. Augustine*—"a work that meets even the strictest formal prescriptions for the genre"—and concluding with *The Scarlet Letter*—"a work that retains no vestige of the self-biographical mode." His goal is "to demonstrate the generic kinship between these formally diverse works by locating them both within a single evolving tradition that arose in the early Middle Ages and arrived at the conclusion of its own internal logic in the nineteenth century."[57] Spengemann believes that in his *Confessions* Saint Augustine "devised three autobiographical forms—historical self-recollection, philosophical self-exploration, and poetic self-expression—from which every subsequent autobiographer would select the one most appropriate to his own situation."[58] In tracing the evolutionary path he argues that each of the three formal strategies autobiographers have used—historical, philosophical, and poetic—is characteristic of (although not necessarily most frequent in) an age to which he assigns it.[59] These three formal strategies reflect "conditions that have led different autobiographers to write about themselves in different ways."[60]

Patricia Spacks attends to how context shapes the focus and substance of autobiographies. In her attempt to explain some of the differences in autobiographies, Spacks starts with a deceptively simple question: "Why do autobiographies now sound so different from those of the nineteenth and eighteenth centuries?"[61] Admitting that the study of modes of justification and of the systematic exclusions might provide insight into answering this question, she turns her attention to "a rather impressionistic view of a general pattern of social change."[62] Her starting point is the observation of the historian Philippe Aries: "It is as if to every period of history there corresponded a privileged age and a particular division of human life."[63] She argues that the eighteenth, nineteenth, and twentieth centuries produced autobiographies that focused on a particular period of life, respectively maturity, childhood, and adolescence.[64] The attention to a particular stage of life, of course, mandated different themes and approaches. So the eighteenth century, with its emphasis on maturity, produced works that focused on what the author had accomplished and done in her life. Nineteenth-century works explored the experiences of childhood, the sense of self during that critical period, and the influences that shaped the author during these early years. The difference in focus between the eighteenth- and nineteenth-century autobiographies is especially obvious in the comparison between men's and women's works during the two periods. Deprived of access to the public realm, women in the eighteenth century often saw their adult lives as periods of restriction and looked longingly back to childhood; in contrast, men savored the freedom and activity of their adult years. In the nineteenth century, with its focus on childhood, the differences between the two sets of autobiographies are less apparent.[65]

Our own century turns its attention to adolescence, a period of defiance and the creation of an identity. Themes of self-discovery and self-invention, of the uniqueness of the individual's experience and inner life dominate in this era.[66] Spacks concludes that the preoccupation of twentieth-century autobiographers with their adolescence and its influence on their lives locates "power

26

and pleasure in this time of life . . . [and] suggests a kind of reconciliation between the eighteenth and nineteenth century view."[67] In short, Spacks argues that the historical era strongly shapes an autobiography: "When one climbs upon a literary stage to perform the self, one chooses the costume, assumes the poses, that the audience of one's own time—and oneself as audience—will recognize."[68] Implicit in Spacks's view is an identification (in the Burkean sense discussed in chapter 1) between author and reader, the communicative bond that I believe undergirds the rhetorical power of autobiographies.

Heidi I. Stull argues for a different set of forces as key shapers of autobiographies. She contends that between 1770 and 1850 "new developments in literature (especially the emergence of the novel) and new trends in philosophy and aesthetics . . . ushered in a new era reflective of a new consciousness" that forced the genre of autobiography to evolve into distinctively different branches.[69] In the classical or conventional autobiography, factual or historical narrative controls the work. Other autobiographers combine "Poetry and Truth," by subordinating their lived experience to artistic goals. Finally, in the autobiographical novel, artistic considerations dominate and subvert the historical impulse. In other words, the tensions between the demands of historical narration and artistic creation have altered over time; the shifting balance between the two impulses have produced different autobiographical forms. According to Stull's view, these changes have been so profound that it is "impossible to accommodate all future so-called autobiographical writings under one single definition without destroying the very concept of autobiography."[70] In essence, Stull believes that as the genre grew and developed, it fragmented into various related though distinctively different forms.

TEXTUALITY AND AUTOBIOGRAPHY

Rather than seeing meaning as a message placed in a work by the author, reader-response critics and deconstructionists have probed the nature of meaning in texts and how it is constructed by the reader as well as the author. Some critics have also questioned the status of the writer within a text. Rather than surveying all the work done in this area, let us examine two representatives of this thinking who explore issues of textuality and meaning from two different angles.

Reader-response critics such as Janet Varner Gunn focus on texts as sites where meaning is created by both the author and the reader. To begin, Gunn disputes "the genre-assumptions of classical autobiography—more accurately, the assumptions of autobiography *theorists*— . . . [about] the self's position vis a vis itself and the world. The self knows itself, according to classical autobiographical theory, from the inside out. That being the case, the self is the best, indeed the only, source of self-knowledge."[71] Gunn rejects this view because it "deports autobiography from the country of vital experience to the desert island of Husserlian reduction or a reified textual system." The kind of self typically assumed in autobiographical theory, she contends, "never *was;* it simply *is*"; and it is better termed the *antibiographical* rather than the autobiographical self.[72]

Gunn prefers to see autobiography as a "cultural act of self reading" with two dimensions: reading done respectively "by the autobiographer, who in effect, is 'reading' his or her life; and by the reader of the autobiographical text," who reconsiders her own life in the light of the encounter with the text.[73] Both acts take place within the "autobiographical situation," which has three constituents: (1) the autobiographical impulse, which "arises out of the effort to confront the problem of temporality"; (2) the perspective, which brings the impulse to language and displays it as a narrative surface; and (3) the response, which includes the reader's appropriation of and relation to the work.[74]

In the context of my study of autobiographies, Gunn's conceptualization of the autobiographical situation presents an intriguing counterweight to Lloyd Bitzer's well-known "rhetorical situation."[75] Bitzer argues that a rhetorical situation has three components: an exigency, an imperfection marked by urgency, which can be alleviated by that discourse; an audience composed of agents of change and to whom the rhetor must address her discourse; and constraints that shape her response to the exigency, which include her own limitations and strengths, the attitudes of her audience, and any other factors that influence how she adapts her discourse. Bitzer's rhetorical situation is material; it is "out there" in the world. The discourse is an attempt to cope with social issues that require communal effort. Oratorical autobiographies, those that will be the focus of this project, are responses to rhetorical situation; in a particular social context the rhetor wishes to shape the reader's view of her life and her ideology.

On the other hand, Gunn's conceptualization of the autobiographical situation sheds light on how the autobiographer crafts her response to a rhetorical situation, opting for the form of an artistically constructed narrative of her life. In oratorical autobiographies, as the author reads her life in time and brings it into narrative, she invites the reader to interpret her story, to find his or her own meaning in it. If the reader finds meaning and establishes a connection with the author by construing the narrated life as revealing some relevant truth, the autobiography achieves rhetorical force. Taken together, Gunn's and Bitzer's views provide a broad view of the full rhetorical transaction: the external rhetorical situation (à la Bitzer) stimulates the production of autobiographical discourse; in that discourse author and reader mutually look for meaning and purpose in their respective lives.

In contrast to Gunn, who sees the autobiography has embodying and then inviting two readings of a life, Paul de Man assaults the very concept of *auto-*

biography. In a predictably provocative essay de Man refutes the alleged referentiality that underlies theories of autobiography as a genre. He asks:

> But are we so certain that autobiography depends on reference, as a photograph depends on its subject or a (realistic) picture on its model? We assume that life *produces* the autobiography as an act produces its consequences, but can we not suggest, with equal justice, that the autobiographical project may itself produce and determine the life and that whatever the writer *does* is in fact governed by the technical demands of self-portraiture and thus determined, in all aspects, by the resources of the medium? And since the mimesis here assumed to be operative is one mode of figuration among others, does the referent determine the figure, or is it the other way around: is the illusion of reference not a correlation of the structure of the figure, that is to say no longer clearly and simply a referent at all but something more akin to a fiction which, then, however, in its own turn, acquires a degree of referential productivity?[76]

In short, de Man argues that the "self" in autobiography is in no sense an image of the author. The generic demands and the textual features of autobiography construct and determine what an author produces. Louis A. Renza reflects a similar view when he notes, "as we learn from instances where fiction mimics autobiography, the narrative by itself formally determines and so takes precedence over the putative, factual orientation of autobiographical references. . . . The autobiographical enterprise occludes the writer's own continuity with the 'I' being conveyed through the narrative performance."[77] Olney describes the French critics:

> But at this point the French critics tell us . . . , the text takes on a life of its own, and the self that was not really in existence in the beginning is in the end merely a matter of text and has nothing whatever to do with an authorizing author. The self, then, is a fiction and so is the life, and behind the text of an autobiography lies the text of an "autobiography": all that is left are characters on a page, and they too can be "deconstructed" to demonstrate the shadowiness of even their own existence.[78]

Thus, autobiography is not a speech act—the narrating of a life—but instead a kind of trope, a literary figure that substitutes a crafted narrative for a lived existence. De Man argues the trope prosopopoeia (personification) governs the autobiographical act: "Prosopopeia, the fiction of an apostrophe to an absent, deceased, or voiceless entity, . . . posits the possibility of the latter's reply and confers upon it the power of speech, is the trope of autobiography. Voice assumes mouth, eye, and finally face, a chain that is manifest in the etymology of the trope's name, *prosopon poien,* to confer a mask or a face (*prosopon*)."[79] Like prosopopoeia, an autobiography invests what is, in reality, an abstraction, an inanimate record of one human's existence, with an illusion of life and humanness. In so doing, an autobiography obscures the very referent (a human's lived experience) it purports to convey. De Man concludes aphoristically: "Autobiography veils a defacement of the mind of which it is itself the cause."[80] In effect, de Man's approach turns attention away from such traditional concerns as the authoritative speaker, intentionality, truth, meaning, and generic integrity toward "the careful teasing out of warring forces of signification within the text itself."[81]

Despite their different angles of vision, the critics discussed in this chapter provide a foundation for this study in at least three areas. First, these critics all see the "I" of the autobiography as a rhetorical construction, the image the author wishes to convey to the world. Thus, they draw attention to the nature and importance of the author's persona in such works. Second, as a group, these works implicitly endorse the idea that different contexts and concerns may have a dramatic impact on how the author crafts her persona. Because works emerge in different eras and from different exigencies, autobiographies bear traces of the situation in which they were written. Social contexts impinge on autobiographers both as exigencies and as constraints to which the authors must respond. In essence, these critics, despite their disparate perspectives, concur in seeing autobiographies as creative rhetorical artifacts, in which authors develop personae and respond to different social forces as they write the stories of their lives.

De Man, Gunn, and other contemporary critics provide another foundation to my rhetorical perspective. Gunn's work, like de Man's, highlights autobiographies as re-creations of lives, with the author not so much reporting on her experiences as shaping and making meaning in them. Moreover, Gunn's analysis draws attention to the reader's role in autobiographies. Rather than being a passive recipient of the narrative, the reader interacts with the material, finding her or his own meaning in the story of another's life. When applied to oratorical autobiographies, Gunn's perspective on the reader's role reflects my concern for the autobiographical pact that provides the identification between author and reader, which is crucial to the work's rhetorical function.

Whatever their theoretical perspectives, previous critical researchers on autobiography have viewed the genre through the lenses of history and/or literature. They have chosen works because of the distinction of the authors or the literary quality of the works. Their attention has been on the qualities of the texts and their relationships to the authors. The perspective in this study, though informed by their work, is quite different. I wish to view one group of autobiographies, those written by movement leaders, as first and foremost persuasive documents. They are, I feel, a complement and supplement to the public discourse and activism of these leaders. Thus, attention will be on the context that produced each work and its relationship to the readers for whom it was intended.

CHAPTER 3

EMMA GOLDMAN AS A LIBERATED WOMAN

A Feminist Writes an Anarchist Life

My life—I had lived in its heights and its depths, in bitter
sorrow and ecstatic joy, in black despair and fervent hope. I had drunk
the cup to the last drop. I had lived my life. Would I had
the gift to paint the life I had lived!

Emma Goldman, *Living My Life*

If I had my life to live over again, like anyone else,
I should wish to alter minor details. But in any of my more important
actions and attitudes I would repeat my life as I have lived it.
Certainly I should work for Anarchism with the same devotion and
confidence in it ultimate triumph.

Emma Goldman, "Was My Life Worth Living?,"
Harper's Magazine

In writing her autobiography, Emma Goldman sought to depict her vibrant experiences as an advocate for anarchist truth. However, from her perspective, the political was intimately and inextricably connected to the personal. Writing to Alexander Berkman, her close friend, she averred that "from the time I entered our movement I had no personal life which did not also reflect the movement, or my activities in it."[1] Candace Falk, one of Goldman's biographers, observed that Goldman did not wish to write "a conventional biography: she would not present the public figure without giving an account of her struggle to realize her *political* ideals in her personal life."[2] Goldman herself perceived the difficulty she confronted in seeking to unite the sometimes disparate strains of her personal and political ideals. "I am writing the life of Emma Goldman, the public person, not the private individual. I naturally want to let people see what one can do if imbued with an ideal, what one can endure and how one can overcome all difficulties and suffering in life. Will I be able to do that and yet give also the other side, the woman, the personality in quest for the unattainable in a personal sense? That's going to be the rub. But I mean to do it."[3] To another friend she admitted that reliving the past had been difficult and painful but insisted that her record might "help the young generation to see that no life is worth anything, which does not contain a great ideal, and which does not bring forth determination to serve it to the uttermost."[4] Clearly, Goldman wanted the work to be the record of an anarchist life, a model of commitment to an ideal. In so doing, she hoped to convey some truth about the human condition, at least as seen from an anarchist perspective.

Goldman was quite clear about whom she hoped to reach. Often contemptuous of "bohemians" and "intellectuals" whom she found pretentious, her target was "the masses." She wrote her longtime friend Agnes Inglis, "I am anxious to reach the mass of the American reading public, not so much because of the royalties, but because I have always worked for the mass."[5] But even as she sought to reach this group, she was doubtful that many persons could appreciate her "agony of soul" throughout her life. Still she hoped to realize both some profits from the book to support herself and some public recognition to facilitate her return to the United States from her unwelcome and difficult exile.[6]

Writing her life story to reach the masses and to garner sympathy for the cause to which she had devoted her entire adult life, she faced the challenge of revealing how anarchism gave both direction and meaning to her existence. If Goldman's goal was to provide a model of the anarchist life, particularly a woman's, the story of her own conversion to the cause was crucial to her rhetorical purpose. To convey the power of her ideal her narrative had to provide some explanation of the factors that attracted her to anarchism and motivated her lifelong commitment.

As readers perused her narrative, they would inevitably test it for coherence and fidelity to see if Goldman offered good reasons for her actions and her commitments. Even a sympathetic reader would weigh the motivations for her views and the factors that contributed to her commitment. In implicitly comparing her reasons with their own understanding of the situation, readers would consider the allure and impact of her new ideology.

Goldman saw her conversion to anarchism as the crucial turning point in her life; she begins her autobiography with that time to show its importance rather than offering the more chronologically typical description of her parental background and childhood. The few details she offers about her life before this event follow her narrative of her conversion. In beginning her autobiography this way, Goldman assumes the rhetorical burden of conveying cogently the "truth" of anarchism, as evidenced in her own conversion, for her readers in order to validate her own continuing commitment to the cause.

The focus of this chapter will be an examination of the lengthy portion (over 175 pages) of Goldman's extensive autobiography that depicts her conversion to anarchism. The reasons for confining attention to this section are twofold. First, this section is crucial to Goldman's larger project. If she is to convey the power of an ideal in a life, she must show readers how she herself became aware of the truth of anarchism. Second, to show the particular problem focused on here—Goldman's failure to provide a rationale for her commitment to anarchism—this section is typical of the book as a whole. Indeed, as I will show later, reviewers of the book when it was published pinpointed this weakness.

The central argument of the discussion that follows is that Goldman's depiction of her conversion to anarchism fails to provide a convincing explanation of her commitment to this controversial doctrine. Although her narrative does give the reader intriguing glances of Goldman as a liberated woman—one reason, I contend, for the renaissance of this book in the wake of the modern feminist movement—her treatment of her conversion experience fails the tests of narrative coherence and fidelity that would help the reader to find in it good reasons for her lifelong commitment.

THE CREATION OF AN ANARCHIST

In writing her life story, Goldman chose to deviate from the chronological structure typical of the form. Believing that her conversion to anarchism was a critical juncture in her life, she begins her narrative by depicting that event. Goldman explains her decision to begin her narrative with her arrival in New York City at age twenty, some four years after her immigration to the United States from Russia. "All that had happened in my life until that time was now left behind me, cast off like a worn-out garment. A new world was before me, strange and terrifying. But I had youth, good health, and a passionate ideal. Whatever the new held in store for me I was determined to meet unflinchingly." [7] The "passionate ideal" was anarchism, and Goldman devotes the first section of her autobiography to chronicling her evolution as an anarchist. Her close attention to her initial commitment to anarchism, her insistence on the significance of the cause to her life, and her expressed intention of showing the power of an ideal in human existence all indicate that she felt her conversion to anarchism could serve as a model for others. But rather than explaining her ideology or tracing the roots of her conversion, Goldman reports that two series of events keyed her changeover to anarchism: her reaction to the trial of the Haymarket anarchists and her relationships with men already deeply committed to the cause. Unfortunately, her narrative of these crucial events provides little guidance for the reader in understanding the allure of anarchism and offers a model of conversion problematic for most contemporary women to follow.

The Haymarket incident involved a group of Chicago anarchists who were tried and executed for allegedly throwing a bomb that killed and injured several policemen after a demonstration associated with a strike at the McCormick Reaper Works. Public and press reaction to the event revealed "a nationwide convulsion of deep-rooted and violent prejudice. A fear of subversion seized the country, triggering a campaign of radical-baiting rarely if ever surpassed."[8] In part because press coverage focused on them as immigrants and in part because of her bitter experiences with businessmen in sweatshops, Goldman identified strongly with the accused. "The violence of the press, the bitter denunciation of the accused, the attacks on all foreigners, turned our [hers and her sister's] sympathies to the Haymarket victims" (7).

When, after a lecture about the men, Goldman approached the speaker Johanna Greie, a prominent socialist, Greie remarked on Goldman's strong emotional reaction. Goldman responded that while she did not know the men, "I do feel the case with every fiber." Greie predicted that "as soon as you learn their ideal . . . you will make their cause your own" (9). Her reaction was intensified by reading Johann Most's accounts in *Die Freiheit*, which "fairly took my breath away" (9). Soon, she tells us, she was reading voraciously about anarchism and "saw a new world opening before me" (10). Despite her mention of this reading, Goldman does not summarize the specific ideas she found so enlightening nor even name the specific sources she perused so eagerly.

Finally the day of what was to be her conversion arrived. Upon learning of the execution of the Haymarket anarchists, Goldman was "in a stupor" until she became so outraged at a woman who called them murderers and endorsed their hanging that Goldman attacked her physically. Exhausted by the emotional strain, she fell into a deep sleep. When she awoke, she felt her life transformed: "The next morning I woke as from a long illness, but free from numbness and depression of those harrowing weeks of waiting, ending in the final shock. I had a distinct sensation that something new and wonderful had been born in my soul. A great ideal, a burning faith, a determination to dedicate myself to the memory of my martyred comrades, to make their cause my own, to make known to the world their beautiful lives and heroic deaths" (10).

To accomplish this ambition, Goldman ended her unhappy marriage and left her family in Rochester to go to New York City to seek out Johann Most, who she felt would guide her in her new task (10). Upon arrival in New York City she had little money, no job, and only three addresses to guide her, among them the location of the offices from which Most edited *Die Freiheit*. Significantly, at first she was equally drawn to socialism and anarchism as populist alternatives to the capitalistic status quo. As her narrative clearly indicates, at this point of vacillation strong male personalities and her sexual attraction to specific men were factors that prompted her exclusive commitment to anarchism. The report of her first evening in New York when she went to hear Most speak about the Haymarket tragedy is representative of her reactions to vehemently committed anarchist men:

His speech was a scorching denunciation of American conditions, a biting satire on the injustice and brutality of dominant powers, a passionate tirade against those responsible for the Haymarket tragedy and the execution of the Chicago anarchists in November 1887. He spoke eloquently and picturesquely. As if by magic, his disfigurement disappeared, his lack of physical distinction was forgotten. He seemed transformed into some primitive power, radiating hatred and love; strength and inspiration. The rapid current of his speech, the music of his voice, and his sparkling wit, all combined to produce an effect almost overwhelming. He stirred me to my depths.(6)

Her report of her subsequent relationship with Most continues in this vein. Throughout she emphasizes intellectual admiration and sexual attraction as the dual bases for her growing commitment to him and, consequently, to his anarchism. At no point in the autobiography does she characterize his anarchist ideology nor evaluate it in contrast to the socialism which she says had also attracted her interest. But even while the "charm of the Most" was upon her, she felt herself also attracted to Alexander Berkman, who was to become her lover and her lifelong friend and colleague. The source of his appeal was "his earnestness, his self-confidence, his youth," which "drew me with irresistible force" (36). When she finally establishes a sexual relationship with Berkman, it is after a meeting at which Most had spoken. She was so stirred by Most's words that she at first could not speak. Then she reports, "my whole body had begun to shake as in a fever. An overpowering yearning possessed me, an unutterable desire to give myself to Sasha [Berkman], to find relief in his arms from the fearful tension of the evening" (36).

While Goldman devotes considerable space to her sexual and emotional reactions to these anarchist leaders in *Living My Life*, she never probes their ideology. This pattern persists up through Goldman's assistance in Berkman's attempt to assassinate Henry Clay Frick as a protest against Frick's handling of the Homestead Strike. Only when she is imprisoned for one year for inciting a riot does she free herself from her intense emotional dependence on these particular men, although a string of other relationships was to follow. As she reports of the imprisonment, "The prison had been the crucible that tested my faith. It had helped me to discover strength in my own being, the strength to stand alone; the strength to live my life and fight for my ideals against the world, if need be" (148). But even this confession is not coupled with a clear explanation of the intellectual forces that compelled her self-perceived maturity.

While the Haymarket events and the attraction to Most and Berkman sealed Goldman's commitment to anarchism, her narrative suggests that a sojourn spent studying nursing in Vienna enriched her appreciation for the ideology. There her most significant experiences involved her reading of "young iconoclasts in art and letters," Friedrich Nietzsche principal among them, and her attendance at Sigmund Freud's lectures on sexual repression. Of Nietzsche she wrote: "the magic of his language, the beauty of his vision carried me to undreamed-of heights. I longed to devour every line of his writings. . . . The fire of his soul, the rhythm of his song, made life richer, fuller, and more wonderful for me" (172). Despite such effusion about Nietzsche's significance for her thinking, which is supported by her frequent references to him in her later speeches and writings, Goldman offers no explanation or even mention of the specific ideas that prompted her response. Freud's lectures made her feel she had been "led out of a dark cellar and into broad daylight," enabling her to grasp for the first time "the full significance of sex repression and its effect of human thought and action" and "to understand myself, my own needs" (173). Certainly, sexual freedom became a distinctive and important feature in Goldman's anarchist propaganda. But here she provides no fuller discussion of those ideas and theories. In short, her reactions to European thinkers, which she insisted excited her and confirmed her commitment to anarchism, are characterized by the same emotional intensity and lack of clear elucidation as her depictions of the Haymarket trial and her initial conversion under the influence of Most and Berkman.

At this point (1896) Goldman at age twenty-seven returned to the United States, where she became even more active as a speaker and writer. By 1901, when she was clearly identified as the principal anarchist propagandist in the United States, her personal version of the ideology had reached its fullest development. These events, up through her return from Vienna, constitute the first 175 pages of her autobiography. But this extensive record of her conversion and growing commitment to anarchism devotes virtually no space to an elucidation of the specific tenets or rational foundations of the ideology. Instead, she repeatedly depicts her conversion as stimulated by intense emotional reactions and sexual attraction.

Conversions to a cause are seldom solely rational. And Goldman's exuberant liberation in the wake of her conversion clearly suggests the powerful effects of the ideology on her life. Still, Goldman was, by her own admission, writing to reach the masses to demonstrate to them the importance and validity of anarchism. Her autobiography, then, can be seen as a model of an anarchist life and can be fairly assessed in terms of how well it serves that function.

A RHETORICAL ASSESSMENT OF GOLDMAN'S AUTOBIOGRAPHY

Public Reception

A close reading of these pages of Goldman's autobiography reveals the contradictions between the tenets of her ideology and her depiction of her experiences. Although she avers that anarchism is a highly rational ideology, her own early experiences with the cause do not support her claim. Indeed, a strong tension emerges between her insistence on the rationality undergirding anarchism and her own formative experiences with it. Such tension does not necessarily indicate that the work was a rhetorical failure. But several strands of evidence indicate that the work failed in Goldman's immediate goals of conveying the intellectual power of her ideology and of facilitating her return from exile.

While none probed the significance of the omission, even contemporary reviewers noted the absence of substantive explanations of her ideology. For example, Ordway Tead in the *Yale Review* praised the work as a "compelling and stirring" portrait but added, "one searches in some bewilderment both for the secret of her impassioned life-long and sacrificial devotion, and for the ideas which were to her 'The Cause.'"[9] Waldo Frank, in the *New Republic*, observed that while Goldman was "a deep, hearty presence . . . she is never the analyst or integrator of her story. . . . In a life so purely dynamic, there is no pause for thought, hence her book's total lack of ideology."[10] Reviewers also praised the work as a vivid picture of an "original personality."[11] None saw it as an effective intellectual statement of her ideology. Other reviewers were more caustic, labeling the book "a thousand dull pages of fornication and fanaticism" or dismissing it as the "love life of an Anarchist."[12] The *New York Sun* reviewer entitled his assessment "The Unmarried Life of Emma and Company or Goldman, Goldman, Goldman Uber Alles." While the London *Morning Post* noted her "chronic egoistic excitation," *Everyman* highlighted her "amorous dalliances."[13] Richard Drinnon in his sympathetic biography of Goldman labeled the autobiography "a work of art," tracing its value to its depiction of living a "meaningful life" rather than its intellectual rigor.[14]

While reviewers' comments are not always sufficient evidence of a work's impact, they are especially significant here. After her trial and deportation for working against emancipation in 1919, Goldman became disillusioned with life in Russia. After escaping she became an expatriate in Europe. However, the loss of the public forum she had enjoyed in the United States frustrated her reform efforts. She began to seek a return to the United States. Goldman needed to influence opinion leaders as well as speak to the masses. Apparently her work did not create the sympathetic endorsement she needed.

Immediate public response was also weak. Although the work was recommended by some critics and librarians and circulated fairly well in some libraries, it sold poorly. Goldman reported that sales were almost "nil," blaming the marketing mistakes of the publisher, and assessed the work as a financial "flop."[15] Certainly sales did not generate enough revenue to aid the financial plight of Goldman and Berkman, an outcome which she admitted made its failure "doubly bitter."[16] The book soon passed out of print. Alix Kates Schulman notes that before the resurgence of interest in her among feminists in the 1970s, Goldman had sunk almost into oblivion and the autobiography was not reprinted until 1970, some nine years after Drinnon's biography.[17] In any case, the work clearly did not stir the reaction among workers that Goldman had hoped it would.

If, as Goldman says, she sought to stimulate interest in her ideology with the work, evidence also indicates that she hoped to facilitate her reentry into the United States from what was a frustrating and increasingly circumscribed exile in France. [18] In this goal the work was almost totally unsuccessful. Goldman was allowed to return to the United States for ninety days in 1934 but was denied permission to remain longer. Moreover, public reaction to her lecture tour was not enthusiastic. She attributed the weak response to mismanagement by her agent, who in turn reported that there was "quite a national anti–Emma Goldman sentiment."[19] But biographer Richard Drinnon concludes that Goldman's lectures were less popular than earlier because the nature of radicalism had changed in the United States and Goldman's ideas seemed "hopelessly old-fashioned."[20]

In essence, then, Goldman's autobiography apparently failed to reach the masses and to stir interest in anarchism. Despite her avowed desire to focus attention on herself as a public figure embodying a rational ideology, her autobiography has consistently been perceived as interesting and worthwhile primarily because of her colorful personality. One of the initial reviewers, a professor of literature at Columbia, perceived this strength in his prepublication assessment: "The book itself, it seems to me, can hardly escape being called a masterpiece. Rousseau's *Confessions* are poverty-stricken in incident and pallid in rhetoric beside this enthusiastic vitality. . . . So far as is humanly possible this strikes me as a complete revelation of one of the most vivid and genuinely vital lives and personalities of our time."[21]

Goldman's autobiography has become quite popular in recent years in the wake of the women's movement. According to some observers, she has become "a veritable password of radical feminism."[22] As one reviewer notes, Goldman "has grown into a cult rather than a historical figure."[23] In some respects, then, Goldman has, after a lapse of many years, reached a large number of women and become a model, not for anarchist thought as she initially hoped, but for women's liberation. Paradoxically, Goldman's autobiography failed as rhetoric to meet the particular exigencies she faced but has reemerged in another era to speak forcefully to the concerns of women of another generation.

Why Goldman's work failed to elicit the response she hoped it would with her contemporaries and yet became a significant force for women years later presents an intriguing question. The answer lies, I think, in considering the divergent impulses that shaped Goldman's writing and the limitations of the genre of autobiography as a tool for ideological persuasion.

THE ROOTS OF GOLDMAN'S RHETORICAL FRUSTRATION

In effect, two distinct forces influenced her creation of the narrative: the tendency toward mythmaking often characteristic of autobiography, and her propagandistic goals. In her case these two forces, exacerbated by her commitment to the individualistic strand of anarchism, created a dynamic that produced immediate rhetorical failure.

If one grants that mythologizing is one impulse underlying autobiography, the question arises as to the nature of the persona Goldman sought to convey. Part of the answer lies in her views on her image of the emancipated woman and on feminist issues to which she devoted five of the twelve essays in her only published collection of anarchist theory. In these essays she argued that puritanism and traditional views were particularly restrictive for women. Emancipation, she proclaimed, must begin in a woman's soul, when she severs "the weight of prejudices, traditions, and customs" so that she can become "human in the truest sense. Everything within her that craves assertion and activity should reach its fullest expression; all artificial barriers should be broken."[24] "The greatest shortcoming of the emancipation of the present day," she wrote, "lies in its artificial stiffness and its narrow respectabilities, which produce an emptiness in a woman's soul that will not let her drink from the fountain of life."[25] Goldman thought contemporary liberated women had denied themselves sexual and emotional outlets. Thus, in her autobiography Goldman seeks to convey an image of herself as a spiritually and emotionally liberated woman. The ability to feel passion, which she saw as missing in contemporary women who sought emancipation, had to be a hallmark of her autobiographical persona. She had to portray herself as the model for that true inner liberation that began "in the spirit." This commitment to passionate involvement and experience led Goldman to accentuate her emotional reactions and sexual encounters in her narrative.

Goldman would see this as a misreading, of course, since her intention was to mythologize herself into the "free spirit" of new womanhood and this entailed documentation of her private, unrepressed sexual life, an aspect of womanhood that she saw as slighted in the intellectualized outlook of so-called emancipated women. Indeed, Goldman's rhetorical persona was an enactment of her anarchist belief in unrestrained personal behavior. However, her failure to elucidate the rationale behind her behaviors left her audience unaware of the relationship between theory and practice. In essence, to be convincing as a model for commitment, Goldman's depiction required her reader to participate enthymematically, supplying the intellectual theories that would validate her activities as ideologically consistent. But she herself provides no guidance as to the nature or source of these ideas. Thus, her activities emerge as emblems of personal flamboyance rather than clear ideological statements.

This is a particularly egregious problem in this work because rationality was, in Goldman's opinion, a hallmark of her anarchism. Labeling anarchism "the great leaven of thought" and the "great, surging, living truth that is reconstructing the world," Goldman insisted that the ideology "urges man to think, to investigate, to analyze every proposition."[26] She repeatedly castigates the majority of persons who are guided by blind allegiances and traditions, not troubling themselves to consider alternatives or to question authority. The revolution she sought to achieve was simply a manifestation of individuals' breaking free from the emotional bonds of tradition: "People are either not familiar with their history, or they have not yet learned that revolution is but thought carried into action."[27]

This rhetorically unfortunate dynamic between creating a persona of unrepressed passion and propagandizing for a rational ideology was exacerbated not only by Goldman's gender, but also by her particular strand of anarchism. In contrast to some anarchists, Goldman emphasized the importance and power of the individual rather than of the revolutionary mass. She saw the individual, who was in the enlightened minority, as the source of all new ideas and social progress. As she phrased it, "the living, vital truth of social and economic well-being will become a reality only through the zeal, courage, the non-compromising determination of intelligent minorities."[28] In another essay she asserted, "The individual is the true reality in life. . . . Man, the individual, has always been and necessarily is the sole source and motive power of evolution and progress."[29] This faith in the individual and the necessity for an ideology to adapt to her needs led Goldman to eschew any specific blueprints or firm recommendations for an anarchist future. She reasoned: "The methods of Anarchism therefore do not comprise an iron-clad program to be carried out under all circumstances. Methods must grow out of the economic needs of each place and clime, and of the intellectual and temperamental requirements of the individual."[30] These views led Goldman to prize and praise her individual experiences and sensations even at the expense of a coherent explication of the specific characteristics of her ideology.

In terms of narrative theory, as we have seen, for her contemporaries Goldman's autobiography falters in its coherence because her depiction of her conversion to anarchism reveals a tension in her thinking between the rationality she sees as essential to her ideology and the persona of the emotionally liberated woman she seeks to convey. Particularly problematic is her depiction of the emotional influence of men in her life. Reading the work without a clear ideological rationale, the reader might perceive Goldman as an immature, emotionally controlled young woman who simply adopts the beliefs of men she admires. While she is clearly sexually liberated, she is still intellectually dominated by males. This point is especially clear in her recounting of her first lecturing experiences as Most's protégée. Only when confronted with the direct question and "clear analysis" of one audience member does she realize she "was committing a crime against myself and the workers by serving as a parrot repeating Most's views" (52). While she concludes that the experience "impressed on me the need of independent thinking," she gives no clear indication of the directions she pursued. Later she is drawn into an assassination attempt on Henry Clay Frick, almost entirely by Berkman's emotional power. Thus, her commitment to anarchism stems more directly from her passionate involvement with men than from some rational, intellectual process.

One might argue that the autobiography complements her earlier published essays, which, to some extent, convey her ideas. But since those had been published some fourteen years earlier and since Goldman explicitly stated her goal of reaching the masses with the message of autobiography, one can reasonably criticize her depiction for its failure to elucidate the intellectual dimensions of her "ideal" and to explain its rational power.

New evidence reveals Goldman's apparent lack of candor in treating her sexual experiences. According to Candace Falk, Goldman withheld details of her longtime relationship with Ben Reitman because they reflected a painful vulnerability and insecurity at odds with her expressed individualism. Instead she depicted a contrast between Reitman's "crude nature and her own refined and civilized character."[31] Thus, her depiction does not do justice to the painful tension she experienced between her ideology of sexual freedom and her own dependency on Reitman.

In terms of narrative fidelity, Goldman's depiction was also problematic for her contemporaries on three fronts. Her model of the liberated woman who exercised great sexual freedom was not a feasible idea for most women in an age when effective birth control was not readily available and when childbirth outside wedlock produced a social stigma that might easily cost one employment and familial support. Goldman herself was spared these problems by a physical condition, one she deliberately chose not to have corrected, which rendered conception impossible. Later in regard to conscription, she demurred from advising young men to resist it because as a woman she was not subject to the penalties they might experience. Yet in creating her rhetorical persona in her autobiography she offered a model that few women could emulate because few had her convenient physical condition. While Goldman never concealed this medical fact, she certainly knew of the limited access to birth control, since she had been imprisoned for explaining publicly the few techniques available. Indeed, one modern critic argues that Goldman "was concerned only secondarily with contraception as a method of women's emancipation," viewing the issue instead as a free speech question.[32] Urging sexual liberation, then, to an audience that might face considerable risks in pursuing it made it difficult for many readers to see her story as representative of their own lives.

Goldman's depiction fails the test of narrative fidelity on a second level. Goldman's model of her own conversion, colored as it was by sexual attraction and emotionality, was clearly ill-suited for some readers. Albert E. Stone, in *Autobiographical Occasions and Original Acts,* indicates the root of this difficulty. Emphasizing that autobiography is a "collective process" in which reader and writer work to understand "a singular past," he notes that "Readers . . . derive deep satisfaction from sharing in the act of memory and imagination which connects a self to the 'extensive totality' of the world."[33] In Goldman's case, her re-creation of her past impeded the reader's perception of her experience as instructive about their own. While he might admire her energy and élan, a male reader would have to defy powerful preconceptions to recommend following Goldman's lead in allowing sexual attraction and emotional reaction to engender ideological commitment. Many "liberated" women were too close to arguments against women's rights based on females' alleged overemotionality to be comfortable with the model Goldman offered. In Walter R. Fisher's terms, Goldman's recounting conveyed much "truth" about her view of the world she perceived but too little "truth" about the human condition, especially for her contemporary audience.

Finally, Goldman's gender was undoubtedly a problem. While public promiscuity was not fully acceptable behavior for either sex in her time, it was especially inappropriate for a woman. Not only did Goldman reveal her sexual exploits, including a ménage à trois, but she also emphasized their importance to her life. So central was sexuality and sexual freedom to Goldman and her ideology that after she describes in detail her frustration with her husband's impotence, she insists: "Together with my own marital experiences they [the lives of relatives] had convinced me that binding people for life was wrong. . . . 'If ever I love a man again, I will give myself to him without being bound by rabbi or the law,' I declared, 'and when that love dies, I will leave without permission'" (36). Such statements were undoubtedly shocking to many and made Goldman's model virtually impossible to emulate because of the opprobrium that was sure to follow and that Goldman herself had experienced.

THE RHETORICAL PITFALLS OF AUTOBIOGRAPHY

The Autobiography Simplex

Goldman's problems in fidelity and coherence stem directly from the fact that she wrote what James Olney terms an "autobiography simplex." Such autobiographies, which include the autobiographies written by Charles Darwin and John Stuart Mill, are governed by a particular metaphor or reflect a single controlling perspective. Each writer in this genre "had his daemon, his personal genius and guardian spirit, a dominant faculty or function or tendency that formed part of his whole self and from which there was no escape." Such writers have "little or no self-awareness, little or no criticism of the assumed point of view. . . . There is the felt assumption in each case that this is the way the thing is said, there is no other way."[34] In contrast, writers in the second genre (the autobiography duplex), those governed by a double metaphor, can appreciate their point of view on their lives as but one way of constructing meaning in existence. Their ability to contemplate their own limitations allows them to "weave together personal allusions in such a way as to create a generalized significance, so that the work becomes, in effect, an autobiography of and for Everyman as a philosophic and spiritual being."[35]

In Goldman's case, her absolute commitment to individualistic anarchism blinded her to other views or possibilities. Herself contemptuous of other ideologies, she did little to educate her reader about her perspective in contrast to other viewpoints. For her anarchism was the great "surging, living Truth"; only the weak-minded or the fearful could fail to perceive its clear superiority. Such an attitude would not be problematic if the ideology or viewpoint in question had broad public support, which anarchism certainly did not. Goldman made no attempt to breach the divide between her own perceptions, her own "truth," and that of her readers. Thomas P. Doherty observes the persistence of this problem in other autobiographies when he notes that the tradition of American autobiographies is ideologically conservative. He concludes that "those autobiographies that are the *least* overtly ideological, paradoxically, seem to have the most forceful and long-lasting influence."[36]

On another level, the writer of an autobiography simplex always risks being perceived as an ideologue because her or his view is transfixed by a single perspective. Rhetorically, such an author confronts substantial barriers to credibility with a general audience if her/his "daemon" is not commonly respected. In Burkean terms, such autobiographers have significant problems in establishing consubstantiality with their audiences. An autobiography simplex may stimulate our admiration for the writer as a person of strong principle while it makes us mistrust her/his wisdom and good sense. This problem becomes acute when the author wants to influence the audience toward her/his ideology. In Goldman's case, which may be typical in this respect, her conscious effort to convey the power of an ideal in human life discouraged identification with her anarchism because of her single-mindedness. In "American Autobiography and Ideology" Doherty notes the tendency of propagandists such as Goldman to write autobiographies simplex and the rhetorical perils of doing so: "Regardless of the ideology, the ideologue who is truly interested in criticizing society and gaining adherents would do well to choose a genre other than autobiography. . . . Especially if the ideology subordinates the individual to the Cause, autobiography is, almost by definition, a self-defeating enterprise. The power of narrative and the reader's natural identification with the autobiographer will nearly always make one care more about the ideologue than the ideology."[37]

Personal Mythologizing and Rhetorical Impact

Living out the tenets of her ideology led Goldman to depict and revel in her individualistic impulses. Like many autobiographers, she was led to paint herself as a larger than life personality; in effect, she created a personal mythology that featured exploits and adventures far beyond the range of most people's experiences. But in testing rhetorical narratives, readers look for characterological consistency that springs from "the reliability of characters, both as narrators and as actors." [38] The autobiographical tendency toward personal mythmaking to which Goldman succumbed creates obstacles for writers in meeting this test. The more flamboyant the writer's life and the less conventional her/his behaviors, the more substantial the barriers she/he faces in developing a rhetorically convincing and characterologically consistent persona. Because autobiographies are most commonly written by public figures, readers usually approach the texts with some perception of the writer's character and ethos. The authors must also overcome any initial perceptions readers have about their characters and personalities. Controversial figures thus face additional barriers in moving beyond their public notoriety.

For some authors, Goldman among them, depicting themselves as free spirits, uninhibited by social conventions, makes an intriguing personal saga but may impede their appeal as models for the reader's own life. Because autobiographies must offer "good reasons," in the sense of Fisher's narrative fidelity, to be effective rhetorically, the ideologies they offer must embody at least some values the audience esteems.[39] The ideology must, to quote Fisher, "constitute the ideal basis for human conduct," and the reader must both wish to emulate the author and be able to do so.[40] Personal mythologizing, which portrays extreme eccentricity, great flamboyance, or dramatic deviation from social conventions, hinders the reader's perception of the author as a role model.

Gender is clearly a factor in the process of personal mythmaking. Recent feminist scholars have noted that historically women have lacked the assertiveness and self-confidence to write works that reflected vibrant, dynamic assertiveness in the public arena. As we will see, both Anna Howard Shaw and Elizabeth Cady Stanton circumvented that challenge by strategically depicting themselves as "womanly" leaders. Both Goldman's ideology and her personality led her to flout such conventions. However, undoubtedly her gender made her assertiveness and flamboyance doubly upsetting to many potential readers among her contemporaries. Women thus must be especially careful in crafting their rhetorical personae in oratorical autobiographies to take cognizance of the limitations that social preconceptions about their gender impose on their narratives. To overlook or ignore these gender-based constraints runs the risk of rendering the work rhetorically ineffective, at least in a short-term effort to elicit support.

While autobiography can be an effective form of public moral argument, autobiographers face distinct, substantial obstacles in constructing compelling narratives. Constrained by historical facts and drawn to personal mythmaking, they can easily write interesting character studies. Producing an effective rhetorical narrative for their contemporaries presents a different challenge. While autobiography may seem an excellent medium for conveying the power of an ideal in a human life, as we see so strikingly in the case of Emma Goldman's *Living My Life*, the humanness, spontaneity, and vitality in the life often undercut the narrative's rhetorical force as ideological argument.

But Doherty's view of the problems facing authors who espouse a controversial ideology in their autobiographies overlooks the power of the personal mythology such authors may create. More radical works may be effective in encouraging individuals to defy social constraints. From this perspective, autobiographies simplex may be very effective as "consciousness raising" tools to stimulate heightened awareness of social constraints. Albert E. Stone, for example, points to the autobiographies of twentieth-century American women, Goldman among them, as a distinctive subgenre because they focus so intensely on the "tensions between old conventions and new circumstances, between rigid social stereotypes, and the urge to define oneself in wider terms." Writers of such works, he maintains, offer "cultural leadership."[41] Goldman's autobiography demonstrates Stone's theory quite clearly: her work has been most popular with persons, especially modern feminists, who relish her spirit of rebellion and have little interest in her anarchist ideology. In essence, Goldman's autobiography created its audience. Its lack of a clear anarchist ideology and her flamboyant, controversial persona in the work have become rhetorical assets in influencing women of a later time. Such personal sagas may—as has Goldman's—become part of the forces that reshape the conventions that constrain them.

Goldman's narrative is, by almost any standard, highly unconventional. She stakes out a vision of womanhood far removed from contemporary notions of decorum for her gender. In the case studies that follow, we will see that other women, who also defied contemporary mores about women's activities, offer more moderate images of modern womanhood. Frances Willard, for example, with deft rhetorical strokes manages to transform her controversial activities and commitments into an image of a progressive woman still loyal to traditional values. Depicting the source of her commitment as deriving from Christian principles, Willard firmly grounds her views in a doctrine already accepted by her followers. In their autobiographies Elizabeth Cady Stanton, Anna Howard Shaw, and Mary Church Terrell enact models of womanhood that also pay allegiance to traditional female values and commitments. Like Willard, they insist that they can remain loyal to home and family while still agitating for the expansion of women's rights and social justice. But unlike Willard, they locate the source of their commitment in their life experiences as they sought to please parents, educate themselves, or lead socially constructive and responsible lives. Although their commitments lack a religious warrant, they are nonetheless grounded in values widely held by Americans. Thus, in a sense, the lives of these women—Goldman, Willard, Cady Stanton, Shaw, and Church Terrell—form a continuum of womanliness: to a varying degree, each woman stretches traditional boundaries. As a group, the recorded lives of these women work to redefine womanliness and to broaden the scope of acceptable activities for their gender.

CHAPTER 4

FRANCES WILLARD AS PROTECTOR OF THE HOME

The Progressive, Divinely Inspired Woman
by James Kimble

May I be brave enough to speak in a womanly
voice my honest word in this behalf.

Frances Willard, quoted in Amy Rose Slagell,
"A Good Woman Speaking Well: The Oratory of Frances E. Willard"

In some respects Frances Willard and Emma Goldman are a study in contrasts. While Goldman struggled to advance a controversial ideology, Willard was at the forefront of what became a widely supported, female-championed cause. While Goldman lived the life of a liberated woman exuberantly, Willard cloaked her assertive leadership style and increasingly radical agenda in the guise of preserving "true womanhood." Both women, however, faced the rhetorical challenges of explaining their commitments to a social agenda and their untraditional activities in its behalf. As is clear from the previous chapter, Goldman chose to highlight her flamboyant life, at the risk of shocking, alienating, and even confusing readers who sought to understand her anarchism through her autobiography. Willard opted for a different, more strategically conservative course: she depicted her commitment as a divine commission and her activities as a response to heavenly inspiration. In fulfilling that commission and responding to that inspiration, she was a progressive woman who cherished many traditional views but simultaneously sought a wider compass for the good works of women.

Willard was perhaps the most powerful and most famous woman in the United States during the closing decades of the nineteenth century. Under her inspired leadership the Woman's Christian Temperance Union (WCTU) grew from a single-issue interest group with little domestic impact to an international tempest of activity, partisanship, and influence.[1] The WCTU's membership rolls under Willard swelled past the combined membership of every other organized woman's group of the time with over two hundred thousand activists.[2] Willard herself visited over one thousand towns in the United States at least once; in her career she spoke before over seven thousand audiences.[3]

Over the many years she led the national and world WCTU, she molded the organization into a tremendous political force. At one point allying the WCTU with the Prohibition Party, she then fostered a national reform coalition that involved the embryonic Populist Party;[4] she even claimed that her organization, composed largely of women without the franchise, had significantly influenced the presidential election of 1884.[5] Summarizing the great scope of Willard's impact, Joseph R. Gusfield, in *Symbolic Crusade: Status Politics and the American Temperance Movement,* describes her as:

> one of those Reformers with a capital "R" who fill the pages of nineteenth century American history. Her motto might well have been, "Nothing new shall be alien unto me." She threw herself into the suffrage movement, the dress reform crusade, the spread of cremation, the vegetarian cause, the kindergarten campaign, and a multitude of other reform interests. After 1890 she added Populism, Fabianism and Christian Socialism to her major concerns. Sparking the campaign for equal rights for women, she learned to ride a bicycle in order to popularize the freer and healthier costume which permitted this form of exercise.[6]

Such a powerful woman in a time of social, economic, and political strictures on everything deemed "womanly" was bound to attract attention, and even to create enemies. Indeed, Willard did see her share of negative opinions. Although she efficiently ran the WCTU as its president from 1879 until her death in 1898, the style and the direction of her leadership were often seriously questioned. On one occasion about two hundred local WCTU branches seceded from the national organization, loudly protesting Willard's—and thus the WCTU's—support of the Prohibition Party.[7] Willard had several semi-public feuds with other WCTU leaders, including J. Ellen Foster, Annie Wittenmeyer, and Mary Clement Leavitt, an old friend who faulted her "in public and accuse[d] her in private of disloyalty and deviousness."[8] In *Frances Willard* biographer Ruth Bordin sympathetically opines that Willard's internal squabbles "were not unusual for a national political leader attempting to hold an uneasy coalition together. In no way could she avoid controversy while operating on so wide a stage."[9]

Criticism of Willard existed outside of the WCTU as well. Her hometown newspaper, the *Evanston Index,* once suggested that her "endorsement of the free silver craze" was "only one of several follies which she has commended to the women who wish to reform humanity."[10] Willard had an ongoing battle with the antilynching crusader Ida Wells Barnett, who publicly claimed that Willard "condoned fraud, violence, murder, at the ballot box; rapine, shooting, hanging, and burning."[11] Willard also found reasons to disagree publicly with Elizabeth Cady Stanton and Elizabeth Boynton Harbert. The suffragist leader Matilda Joslyn Gage called Willard "the most dangerous person on the American continent today."[12]

It is surprising, however, that Willard did not receive even greater levels of opprobrium from her contemporaries. Many of her projects were more than simple reforms; they invited the label "radical." In particular, Willard developed an intense support for the "woman question," and by 1881—several years before the creation of the National American Woman Suffrage Association (NAWSA)—she had convinced the WCTU to support "Equal Franchise, where the votes of women joined to those of men can alone give stability to temperance legislation."[13] She persuaded the Union to give its support to the Prohibition Party after she became a member of its executive committee and openly campaigned for its 1888 national candidates.[14] And in 1886 Willard established friendly relations between the WCTU and the nation's first labor organization, the Knights of Labor.[15]

A study of Willard's life suggests that these risky endeavors formed part of her lifelong struggle against strictures on nineteenth-century women—what Barbara Welter calls "the Cult of True Womanhood."[16] At least part of Willard's success in advancing her causes while facing such a constraint-filled environment is attributable to her speaking abilities. Karlyn Kohrs Campbell agrees, arguing that "Willard's power came from her leadership ability which, in turn, was directly related to her skill as a speaker."[17] Willard was indeed a spellbinding orator, receiving rave reviews almost wherever she spoke.[18] Many of her audience members must have come to see her in a positive light in spite of her controversial stands.

But Willard's voice was not the only available medium for advancing her causes. In 1889 at age fifty she published her autobiography, nearly seven hundred pages of anecdotes, philosophy, speeches, and diary entries. *Glimpses of Fifty Years: The Autobiography of an American Woman* sold well, with the initial printing of fifty thousand copies exhausted in only a few months.[19] An 1894 version, edited by Frances E. Cook, emerged in England while Willard was there promoting the World's WCTU.[20]

The autobiography appeared as Willard was facing much criticism. The year 1889 capped a hectic period in a political maelstrom for the WCTU and its president. Biographer Mary Earhart argues that the last few years of the 1880s found Willard in a "cross-fire of criticism," with the temperance leader "beset by critics both without and within the Union and without and within the Prohibition party."[21] The 1888 WCTU convention, which took place a few months before Willard began to write her life story, is described in the minutes as a "trying meeting."[22] Slagell, moreover, suggests that "unrest concerning Willard's political commitments continued within the WCTU until the 1889 convention," the year her autobiography was published.[23]

Clearly the situation Willard faced as she wrote her autobiography was filled with challenges to her leadership.[24] As the WCTU's well-known and charismatic leader, she knew sustained criticism of her could quickly tarnish the Union itself and, ultimately, endanger its work. Thus, at age fifty, still vigorous and active, she wrote her life story. This autobiography, offering "glimpses" of her life, became one of Willard's primary vehicles in answering the negative perceptions of thousands of contemporaries and in reassuring her supporters. Moreover, it crystallized her public image as a womanly leader.

My central argument in this chapter is that Willard used her autobiography as a means of personal re-creation, responding to negative views in two primary ways. First, she reassured her supporters by redefining her goals. Many of Willard's contemporaries viewed her as possessing blatantly political aims. In response, Willard used the autobiographical form's narrative basis as a resource to embed her controversial aims within God-inspired actions to protect the home. Second, Willard defended her persona by depicting herself as a progressive woman. Willard's critics sometimes castigated her image for her violation of women's traditional social boundaries. Accordingly, Willard used her autobiography to "feminize" her persona. In particular she used her life story to frame herself as hesitant and self-effacing.

In accomplishing this re-creation of her aims and her persona, Willard underscored her supporters' view of her as a womanly woman. To explicate how she re-created her public image, what follows explores, in turn, Willard's autobiographical reconstruction of her purpose and of her public persona. The concluding section returns to the idea of autobiographies as re-creative tools, contrasting both the strengths and weaknesses of Willard's autobiography with Emma Goldman's later life story.

Purpose: God-Inspired Home Protection

During the 1880s Willard worked hard to move the WCTU beyond its original sole interest in temperance work. Taking one of her slogans—"Do Everything"—almost literally, the White Ribbon Women involved themselves in nearly every imaginable reform, including women's clothing, free kindergarten, prisons, age of consent laws, delinquent girls, and labor-saving devices for the home.[25]

Willard's interest in controversial political issues, however, created her greatest challenge. Not only did she openly espouse woman suffrage, she also campaigned in elections, advised politicians, and was generally outspoken in a sphere that was clearly masculine. Most contemporary Americans resisted the idea of women's participation in politics.[26] Many of them, as would be expected, questioned Willard's motivation, hinting that she was interested only in the politics and not in helping others. Republicans, for example, "blamed Willard and the WCTU for stealing enough votes from their party in 1884 to guarantee the election of Democrat Grover Cleveland."[27] Willard herself wrote that her "advocacy of the Prohibition party" had "seriously interfered with what friends call a 'rising popularity'" (453). And one editorialist complained that "Miss Willard wants the ladies who are banded together to promote the cause of temperance, to go off on a tangent to take up every crack-brained doctrine the conservative and temperate elements of the nation repudiate as mischievous and socialistic."[28]

Willard's first challenge in re-creating her life story was, therefore, to answer charges that she was meddling too much in politics. In a related way she sought to strengthen her ties to her sympathizers. Although any observer could see that many of Willard's actions were political, the autobiography allowed her to concentrate on transforming her goals away from the political and into the divine. More succinctly, Willard redefined her clearly political activities into a God-inspired mission to protect the home.

Glimpses works this direction in two ways. On one level, the autobiographical narrative permits her to present a powerful source of motivation; she depicts major political decisions and actions as stemming from God's counsel. On a second level, Willard shrewdly uses the chronology inherent in narrativity to frame her political goals within the context of home protection.

Initially, as Willard re-creates the trajectory of her life, she simultaneously self-discloses intimate descriptions of God-inspired motivation for her major decisions even as she makes those decisions. When Willard describes her agonizing struggle over a career choice, for example, the objective setting of her decision for temperance work—a hotel room in Portland, Maine—frames her description of how the Bible guided her choice. In that hotel room Willard recalls: "[I] wondered 'where the money was to come from' as I had none, and had mother's expenses and my own to meet, I opened the Bible lying on the hotel bureau and lighted on this memorable verse: Psalm 37:3, '*Trust in the Lord, and do good; so shalt thou dwell in the land, and verily thou shalt be fed.*' That was a turning point in life with me. . . . here came clinching faith for what was to me a most difficult emergency" (337–38).

Her decision made, Willard becomes president of Chicago's local WCTU in 1874, testing her faith by not accepting compensation and often going hungry. Appropriately, Willard the author of the autobiography retrospectively gives the narrative Willard the noble thought that she is "simply going to pray, to work and to trust God" (343). The same Chicago group sends her on several trips; in 1876 she pauses in Ohio, where God tells her to support woman suffrage. According to the text, "while in Columbus for a Sunday engagement, [I] remained at home in the morning for Bible study and prayer. Upon my knees alone, in the room of my hostess, who was a veteran Crusader, there was borne in upon my mind, as I believe, from loftier regions, the declaration, 'You are to speak for woman's ballot as a weapon of protection to her home and tempted loved ones from the tyranny of drink,' and then . . . there flashed through my brain a complete line of argument and illustration . . ." (351).

Later, when Willard splits with evangelist Dwight Moody over women's involvement in spreading God's word, she invokes her belief that God ordained women as Gospel workers. After "a whole summer of thought and earnest prayer for wisdom," she writes: "I firmly believe God has a work for them to do as evangelists, as bearers of Christ's message to the ungospeled, to the prayer-meeting, to the church generally and the world at large, such as most people have not dreamed. It is therefore my dearest wish to help break down the barriers of prejudice that keep them silent" (360).

Obviously, for many contemporaries the political activism implied in these revelations might have invited the very charges to which Willard had to answer. But Willard's primary audience of Christian women would have found this Christ-like persona full of, in Walter R. Fisher's term, narrative probability.[29] This probability, or sense of internal consistency and coherence, makes Willard's political activism more palatable because her motivation stems from divine inspiration.

Willard creates this consistency in her subtle blending of narrative elements. She depicts herself as a Christian answering God's private call, a claim that is hard to prove. Shrewdly, however, she self-discloses these private moments in the midst of narrative descriptions of events. The resulting text seamlessly blends historical fact and self-reported divine inspiration. A less subtle author might have boldly claimed to be God's chosen messenger. But Willard's careful mixture of narrative context creates an overall image of a dutiful Christian answering her calling in the midst of life's everyday travails, an image that would have eased many doubts about the veracity of her revelations.

Willard is careful, too, to draw upon the connection with her reading audience. These revelatory sections arrive after many pages of personal musings and spirit-filled self-disclosure. By the time Willard claims that God directly motivated her to become a temperance and suffrage worker, she has established a close bond with her primary reading audience. The effect, again, is to solidify her readers' sense of consistency as she effectively answers charges of overt political activism by transforming her political aims into divine work.

On a second level, *Glimpses* refutes potential charges of political activism by contextualizing her purpose within work for home protection. In effect, she subsumes her public efforts into a larger quest that is exhibited as more important and sacred than political aspirations. Her primary strategy here is to intertwine inventively the well-known theme of "home protection" into her narrative, often in unexpected places.

Other scholarly works have discussed Willard's rhetorical uses of "home protection" in her oratory.[30] Her autobiography, however, finds a deeper use for this inventive metaphor. The first portion of *Glimpses* focuses on Willard's childhood life. Her depiction of the Wisconsin homestead, Forest Home, is almost idyllic. The description reveals a type of home that the activist Willard, unmarried, living only with other women, and constantly on the road for the WCTU, could no longer claim as her own except in memory.

Being vulnerable to criticism of her unorthodox home life as an adult, Willard relies on the home her parents wrought to show readers that she is a worthy worker for home protection. Here the power of chronology inherent in autobiography emerges to help Willard contextualize later, more activist sections. The early portion of her autobiography essentially serves as a concretization of "home," the kind of home that deserves "protection." This concrete vision of home in effect frames the remainder of the chronology, turning apparently innocuous reminiscences of a happy and wonderful environment into arguments for the activist Willard's rootedness as a proponent of "home values."

Willard's early description of Forest Home is filled with incidents typical of a happy childhood. Indeed, she is often explicit about the utopian nature of her life there. Describing the "magic tie of home love and loyalty," she writes of the farm that "as years passed on, we learned to love it more and more, and never thought of being lonesome" (13, 17). When a visiting friend said, "She should think we would get lonesome, away down there in the woods," Willard's narrative suggests that "we took great exceptions, for we had begun to think that 'Forest Home' was the 'hub of the universe,' and to pity everybody who didn't have the pleasure of living there" (18). Appropriately, one of the aphorisms that Willard sprinkles on each chapter's title page recommends that the reader "keep near to thy childhood, for in going from it thou art going from the gods" (xvii). Reflexively following this advice, later sections of her text hearken back to the theme of home, a theme which narratively points back to the idyllic descriptions of Forest Home.

Immediately after she becomes a local WCTU president, for instance, Willard exclaims her happiness that she "was counted worthy to be a worker in the organized Crusade for 'God and Home and Native Land'" (342). The "loftier regions" revelation, described above, has God telling Willard to use the ballot to protect home and loved ones (351). In telling readers of the WCTU's endorsement of woman suffrage at its 1881 convention, Willard says, "at Boston the ballot for woman as a weapon for the protection of her home was indorsed [sic]" (371). And when she summarizes the aims of the WCTU, she writes: "Its aim is everywhere to bring woman and temperance in contact with the problem of humanity's heart-break and sin; to protect the home by prohibiting the saloon, and to police the state with men and women voters committed to the enforcement of righteous law" (474).[31]

Willard did not herself have a home that listeners to her many speeches could identify as traditional and worthy of protection. Readers of her autobiography, however, are able to feel the effects of Willard's Forest Home throughout the long text. "Home protection," in other words, is not an empty slogan. The phrase is, instead, a heartfelt admonition from a woman who has not only lived in such a home but whose very life story is a search to protect similar ones. Each reference to "home protection" in Willard's autobiography serves as a reminder not of her untraditional activist home but of her child-hood home, an image so effectively based in the autobiography's chronology that the invocation of "home" becomes an argument in its own right.

"Home protection" in *Glimpses* serves a parallel function to Willard's divine inspiration; both provide good reasons for her work. By casting Willard as an earnest heroine whose various activities all aim at protecting the home, the autobiography complements the divine nature of Willard's motivation by trans-forming her sometimes controversial public activities into inspired efforts on behalf of the American home. In establishing just what "home" is, then, Willard gives "home protection" a mythic sanctioning power that complements the force of her divine inspiration. When she uses that sanction later in the political section of her text, the term subsumes the political actions by giving them a mythic purpose that is noble and important for readers of the autobiography.

By convincing readers that God was her motivation for actively working on behalf of home protection, Willard transformed what many would have called "political meddling" into "God-inspired protection of the home." No doubt many who had only heard of Willard and her work were surprised by this depiction. However, convincing a surprised reading audience that she was working on God's behalf to protect the home was not sufficient. The other part of her twin struggle against a controversial public image involved transform-ing the nature of her persona.

PERSONA: A PROGRESSIVE WOMAN

As a powerful woman in a time when powerful women were often suspect, Willard had to struggle continually against the possible perception that she might be "manly," a strong nineteenth-century epithet.[32] Working within a context in which many were "opposed to strong-minded women, weak-minded men, and codfish balls, on general principles," Willard often had to work against the immediate reaction that she was "one of God's creatures who had stepped out of the sphere in which her Creator placed her and taken upon herself duties belonging solely to a man." [33]

Writing an autobiography could have compounded Willard's problem. Her message of social progress on several fronts was persuasive to many, but it was too easily rendered useless when auditors rejected the messenger's sex before understanding what she had to tell them. In writing her life story, Willard further threatened to brand herself as "manly." Traditionally the writ-ing of one's life story belonged in the masculine domain; men, after all, were those whose lives were deemed to be appropriate for activities worth record-ing and of interest to others. Women's lives were to be domestic and thus unworthy of being remembered in an autobiography. A woman publishing her life story was by definition trespassing in masculine territory, both by leading a life that others would want to know about and by demonstrating boldness in writing about that life.

Willard's second challenge in capturing her life for contemporaries and for posterity, then, was crafting her persona. Prompting readers to see her as God's agent was only part of Willard's strategy. At a time when Christian women were to be submissive and meek, Willard's public assertiveness even in her struggle for the home required some defense. To make her message fully persuasive, in other words, she needed to convince readers that she remained "womanly" in spite of apparent violations of the feminine sphere. Willard thus depicted herself as a progressive woman, one who had lived an interesting life and who had written her story for publication, but also one who remained essentially feminine. She knew that readers would recognize in her active life an extraordinary woman, an image that Emma Goldman would later share. Willard's strategy in creating the image of a *progressive* woman, however, immediately distinguishes *Glimpses* from Goldman's life story. Goldman's flamboyant career as narrated in *Living My Life* emerges in vivid, almost exhibitionistic detail. Willard, in contrast, chose to downplay her extraordinary image by projecting a more traditional persona. Accordingly, Willard carefully eschewed any hints of masculine traits in her text and concentrated on creating a feminine persona.

Glimpses works ingeniously to give Willard several layers of femininity. The form of the book itself is telling. Printed in dark and light shades of green, the original front and inside covers are decorated in designs of ribbons, flowers, and leaves. The frontispiece pictures Willard in partial profile, blouse decorated with frills and brooch, her hair pulled back. Other illustrations throughout the book are framed in flowery designs, banners, or ribbons; some picture Willard's friends and mother (all women except for a group of male editors) or show places and objects from her life. She even includes a "children's page" and a "facsimile" of her first childhood writing assignment, entitled "The Kitten" (512, 680, 695–697).

In content, Willard also concentrates on deemphasizing what might be perceived as masculine. Although many readers would have wanted to know about her forays into politics and power (information with which Goldman accommodated her audience), Willard instead emphasizes her childhood experiences and more youthful days. Writing initial sections entitled "A Welcome Child" and "A Romping Girl," she fills pages with diary entries describing her childhood games with siblings, her relationship to her parents, and life on their isolated Wisconsin farm. Later sections profile her teaching career, philosophy, and experiences, topics certainly within the range of contemporary women's sphere. Willard does not reach her work as a speaker or in the WCTU until the halfway point of the book; these two sections then abruptly end as the work descends into a dozen-odd "silhouettes," topical essays that Willard apparently could not fit into the main text. All told, in a book of nearly seven hundred pages she devotes only about one-fifth of her content to any experiences that could be deemed "manly."

While *Glimpses*'s form and content encompass effective rhetorical strategies, Willard's efforts to build a feminine persona are furthered most by her use of a feminine style. Kohrs Campbell suggests that early feminists developed a specialized feminine style to adapt to the rhetorical "demands of the podium."[34] Estelle C. Jelinek similarly argues that women developed distinctive substantive and stylistic approaches to autobiographical writing.[35] These two versions of style intersect in *Glimpses,* a text both rhetorical and autobiographical.

The particular feminine style that Willard develops in her autobiography is marked by both narrative discontinuity and strategic self-effacement. The key word in the title is immediately suggestive: *Glimpses* marks the text as one written not chronologically but haphazardly. True to Jelinek's argument, *Glimpses* is discontinuous in that it is consistently "episodic and anecdotal."[36] While the narrative is roughly chronological through the first five hundred pages (unlike Goldman's autobiography, which begins with the author's conversion and then flashes back into the past), *Glimpses*'s chronology often fades from view. "Willard," confirms Jelinek, "constantly interrupts the narrative with letters, articles, speeches, selections from her voluminous journal, and even contributions by siblings, parents, and friends."[37] Willard's narrative, then, even as it uses the resources of chronology to contextualize important events, simultaneously breaks with the traditional "manly" autobiography, typically linear in its chronological development. Within the discontinuous narrative, Willard depicts herself as self-effacing and sometimes reluctant to assume leadership, qualities consistent with the contemporary expectations of women. Her prefatory remarks suggest that writing the book was not her idea but was planned by other leaders of the WCTU. A publisher's note in the English edition claims that "this Autobiography was written at the official request of the 'White Ribbon Women.'"[38] Others, too, apparently asked Willard to write the text. In her words, "I have been asked for it—not once, but many times—by numerous friends, known and unknown, in England and America."[39] Willard cannot be accused of manly egoism, for she would presumably never have written her life's story unless asked by others to do so.

Willard continues to exhibit self-effacement as she narrates the details of her life. She recounts the time when Chicago's local WCTU elects her its president. She is offered a salary though the group cannot afford it, and Willard's response is typical of her narrative portrait throughout: "'Ah,' thought I, 'here is my coveted opportunity for the exercise of faith,' and I quietly replied, 'Oh, that will be allright!' and the dear innocent went her way thinking that some rich friend had supplied the necessary help. . . . But this was not true" (342).

A few years later Willard becomes well-known enough to challenge Annie Wittenmeyer for the National WCTU's executive leadership. In two separate instances (1874 and 1877), however, she demurs, arguing in the first instance that "I was but a raw recruit, and preferred to serve in the ranks" (350). In the second instance, though Willard clearly wanted to be the WCTU president,[40] and though contemporary newspapers apparently reported that she had peevishly said, "Nothing but a unanimous choice would induce me to accept the position," Willard claims that the "facts" of the situation were otherwise. In her words: "I rose and said I would not allow myself to come forward as an opposing candidate when the President of the society, a much older woman than I and one who had borne the burden for some years, was in the field, and I withdrew my name" (368). Despite Willard's withdrawal, others knew of her ambitions, and she received thirty-nine votes, only twenty-one fewer than Wittenmeyer received. Significantly, her autobiography does not record the near-successful challenge; readers receive the impression that her withdrawal was complete, an image consistent with the self-effacing focus of her feminine style.

In all, *Glimpses* "feminizes" Willard's persona in several ways. Using form, content, and a feminine autobiographical style characterized by discontinuity and self-effacement, the autobiography diligently works to transform her. No longer is she an assertive violator of man's sphere, a "manly" woman driven by ambition to leave her appropriate space. She becomes instead a progressive woman, a persona that acknowledges her accomplishments but implicitly proves that she is essentially feminine. Simultaneously, her autobiography's depiction of active work for the divine protection of the home re-creates what many would have called "political maneuvering" into "God-inspired protection of the home." In purpose and persona, then, *Glimpses* performs an amazing re-creative function for Willard, an accomplishment that would be difficult to achieve in a speech or expository essay. The effects of this re-creation, I believe, were felt not only in her personal image but in the image of the WCTU with which she was so closely associated.

AUTOBIOGRAPHIES AS SELF RE-CREATION

I have observed that Frances Willard faced a volatile rhetorical situation when she crafted her autobiography. As would be expected, Willard used her oratorical skills to address that situation. She concluded the fractious 1888 WCTU convention, for example, by telling the assembly: "We are now technically adjourned. Whatever we may feel in our hearts, or not feel; whatever we may have in the way of difference or agreement, I believe every woman here is a Christian woman and has a great kindness toward all the others here, and can say from her heart 'God be with you till we meet again.'"[41] One year later Willard's WCTU presidential address seemed markedly different. Miller speculates that the change—"more spiritual in quality, less pragmatic and action oriented"—may be attributed to the trauma associated with her fiftieth birthday, the milestone that had occasioned her life story in the first place.[42] In these and other ways Willard used her considerable oratorical skills to address a challenging time in her life.

Glimpses of Fifty Years, however, also served as a significant resource for Willard to respond to her volatile situation. The text worked in clever ways to transform her from a potential pariah into a celebrated leader. In particular, Willard's re-creation of her goals and her persona combined to create a compelling rhetorical vision for her primary reading audience.

Glimpses works actively to distance Willard's aims from cries of political maneuvering and to re-create them as divine goals designed to protect the home. At the same time, the narrative works to re-create Willard's persona from that of an "unwomanly" woman to that of a progressive woman proud of her accomplishments but still essentially feminine. These re-creations of aims and persona suggest that *Glimpses* crafts a rhetorical vision for its readers. In this vision Willard becomes God's agent, feminine and fallible but also divinely commissioned on a noble quest to protect the home. At no point, of course, does this re-created image emerge in its entirety. Instead, the text works in myriad and dispersed ways: here building an attractive view of the home; there inserting an example of self-effacement; here writing of a personal encounter with the divine. However, these many small sections work together, drawing upon the powerful resources of autobiography to craft, almost invisibly, a completely re-created portrait.

This rhetorical vision, all the more effective for its subtle nature, would have reverberated in a particularly compelling way for Willard's WCTU followers. Unlike Emma Goldman, Willard had a substantial, ready-made audience for her book. Most of this audience, already committed to Willard and to Christian duty, would not have been searching for flaws or disingenuous statements. Instead, these readers would have found confirmation of their belief in the WCTU and a strengthening of the tie between the union and Willard.

An even wider audience of women would have found Willard's rhetorical vision compelling. To be sure, no one would have suggested that Willard was "ordinary." But *Glimpses*'s rhetorical efforts would have made her example more approachable for the average woman. Each reader could, in her own household, do what she could to join Willard on the mythic quest to protect the home. Moreover, each reader could come to see herself as truly feminine despite any "activist" tendencies. Finally, each reader could come to see herself as doing God's work, perhaps on a smaller scale than the WCTU president's work, but divine work just the same.

That Willard's rhetorical vision was well received seems evident in the autobiography's many reviews. Several writers, for instance, seemed to be convinced of the divine sanction for Willard's purpose. One suggested that the autobiography "is simply the story of a life devoted to making the lives of others brighter, and better, and happier, and its very singleness of aim and earnestness of purpose, makes the record as readable as it is enjoyable, elevating, and instructive."[43] The reviewer for *The Queen* felt it "must quote the proud, frank words with which this masterful, useful woman closes a book instinct with practical Christianity, animated with a fervent religious spirit."[44] Another reviewer believed that "in the great world movement of Christian women she is one of the most valiant and able of captains. Those who miss this book miss a great and noble inspiration."[45] The *Weekly Sun* reviewer was more thoughtful: "You cannot rise from the perusal of Miss Frances E. Willard's autobiography without a feeling of added respect for that remarkable woman. You may disagree absolutely—if not with her aims, at least with her methods for achieving them; but you cannot help rendering homage to her transparent honesty, her rectitude of purpose, and the unmistakable sincerity of her convictions."[46]

Reviewers also seemed eager to accept Willard's feminine persona. Many were explicit supporters of her cause and had viewed her sympathetically from the start. Others, however, were won over by her depiction. "Agreement with all her sentiments, actions, and aims is not to be expected," wrote one, "but the frank and unaffected manner in which the autobiography is written to some extent disarms criticism." Although, the reviewer continues, "it is the life story of a strenuous worker . . . the note of femininity is present throughout, and we see the pale-faced, nervous, energetic little woman struggling against great odds."[47]

The *Glasgow Herald* reviewer wrote that "however prejudiced a reader may be against her opinions and methods, he will hardly . . . assert that the public life of an agitator has injured her true womanliness."[48] Finally, the *London Weekly Sun* suggested that "to those of us who had the impression of Miss Willard as a woman of a severely austere type portions of this autobiography will come as a surprise."

Willard's success in refurbishing her public image, however, did not end with contemporary readers of her autobiography. For students of history Willard remained a quasi-saint for decades. Nearly a dozen full-blown biographies cover her active life of reform.[49] Most are essentially hagiographies, a few early ones actually naming her "St. Frances."[50] Bernie Babcock's 1902 work is an example of a biography that seems amazingly positive. Not content to suggest that Willard's life was a mere blessing on humanity, Babcock writes, "in the great warfare raging at fever heat between the invisible forces of good and evil, the Master Potter, whose handiwork is the constellations of the universe, had need of a chosen vessel, and although she knew it not, He had long been molding Frances Willard for her mission."[51] Another example is Florence Witt's 1898 biography: "Probably no woman's death has ever before thrilled the land with such a universal pang of sorrow, and not only in America and Great Britain, but all over the civilised world, the great leader of womanhood was known and loved. Everyone who understood and appreciated the beauty and Christlikeness of the life which had closed, realised that the world was the poorer because she had left it—the richer because she had trodden its paths, had loved, and toiled, and sorrowed upon it" (137–38).[52]

Two later biographies—Earhart in 1944 and Bordin in 1986—have been much more objective, criticizing Willard's status as a "saint" and suggesting that she was racist and craved fame.[53] The significant difference between these two more objective depictions of Willard and the virtual hagiographies is that the earlier biographies—most written within twenty years of Willard's death—rely almost exclusively on *Glimpses* for their primary research.[54] Willard's autobiography, then, showed its powerful effects not only on reviewers, but also on those who recorded her life for later generations. For when biographers rely strictly on *Glimpses* (or on other writers who relied strictly on it), their portraits of Willard are overwhelmingly positive, clearly showing a complete transformation of both purpose and persona. But when later biographers use other sources in addition to the autobiography, Willard's halo dims and her autobiography's re-creative powers lessen.

In achieving this successful re-creation, Willard's autobiography clearly goes two steps beyond her typical platform speech. Except for her occasional WCTU convention addresses, recorded dutifully in the organization's records, the majority of Willard's speeches were ephemeral for the people who heard her. She spoke before an audience, was convincing, and left town for her next engagement. Meanwhile, her rapt listeners found their recollections of Willard and her persuasive nature waning with the months and years until she was a distant memory.

Glimpses, in contrast, was far from ephemeral. Eagerly purchased by an appreciative public, the autobiography could be read and even reread for increased understanding or pleasure. Willard's contemporaries could peruse her autobiographical transformation at their leisure, a far cry from the too often passing impact of her oratory. Moreover, when many in Willard's audiences—and Willard herself—had passed away, the autobiographical text was still extant, conveying her desired image to readers new and old. Biographers, scrambling to locate reliable sources on her life, found a resource in her own life story, a seemingly innocuous remembrance of a feminine heroine as God's agent on a mythic quest, a story—perhaps unwittingly—that they passed along to new generations.

Glimpses's transformative effect presents an interesting counterpoint to Goldman's *Living My Life*. Both narratives offer portraits of their authors that are unquestioned and ideological, the type of story James Olney describes as autobiography simplex.[55] But while Goldman relies on an ideology with little grounding in her readers' experiences, Willard relies on a Christian ideology. *Glimpses* casts Willard as God's own agent, not meddling in politics but obediently doing his will even as she maintains her femininity. Willard's readers, many of them WCTU members accepting of the Christian basis of her self-characterization, found this creation convincing and endorsed her re-creation.

From a theoretical perspective, Willard's autobiography sheds light on the views of Janet Varner Gunn and Paul de Man discussed in chapter 2. In particular, Gunn asserts that autobiography involves two acts of reading: the author reads her life in retrospect and the audience member reconsiders her own life in the light of the revelations in the text. As we have seen, Willard depicts her life as determined by her obedience to God's will; she sees her efforts, however unpopular or controversial, as responses to divine inspiration. Sympathetic readers, in turn, are both reassured by Willard's implicit defense of her actions and potentially empowered in their own lives; they too can see their activities as fulfilling a divine mission. What matters in this dual transaction is less the accuracy of the historical facts of Willard's life or even her motivations. Rather the author creates a rhetorical fiction under the guise of giving history, while the sympathetic female reader uses that fiction to enlighten her understanding of her own existence.

Willard's text also speaks to de Man's concern that autobiography as a genre may obscure the very person it seeks to reveal. While de Man and others seem to see this as a weakness, they may overlook the rhetorical importance of the created and even artificial persona in a text. As Willard's work suggests, the autobiographical form can artfully re-create or transform a public image. Thus, the form's necessary defacement of the author, to borrow de Man's language, may enhance the author's rhetorical goals. In Willard's case, the artifice of the author *in* the text is a powerful rhetorical tool for the author *of* the text.

Willard's autobiography shows great ingenuity and creativity. As an author she effectively negotiates the tension between the impulse to create personal myth often typical in an autobiography and the requirement of her role as a movement leader that her life be imitable by her followers. In particular, by grounding her mythic quest in divine will, Willard maintains her status as a heroine but empowers readers who, like she, believe that in God all things are possible. Although she writes an autobiography simplex, with her ideology as its only viewpoint, she reveals that viewpoint as God's, and thereby she gives it, and herself, transcendent authority for at least one group of readers. Importantly, her followers can be empowered by the same divine mission if they take her life and experiences as a paradigm of obedience to Divine will.

Moreover, Willard shows that writers can use autobiography to address immediate rhetorical exigencies. In contrast to Elizabeth Cady Stanton, Anna Howard Shaw, Emma Goldman, and Mary Church Terrell, Willard writes her life story after only fifty years. Her relatively youthful age and the troubled months leading up to her text's appearance suggest that her autobiography was a timely answer to immediate problems. Willard's objectives were in trouble because of the controversy growing around her; *Glimpses* was one effort to re-create herself and the cause she represented into acceptable alternatives for a specific audience. As with many writers of autobiography even today, Willard's life story served an immediate need; the popularity of her autobiography seems to show that she was at least partially successful in meeting that goal.

These conclusions suggest that Frances Willard's *Glimpses of Fifty Years* shows some of the power of the autobiographical form. Her text, even in its unwieldy, disjunctive format, remains a monument to her indomitable will and creative ideas, albeit a monument that is difficult to see in the current milieu. Willard saw in autobiography a force that could change her image and enhance the image of her organization. That she succeeded in convincing many suggests not only the strength of her particular approach, but also the power of the form with which she recorded her narrative life.

CHAPTER 5

ELIZABETH CADY STANTON
AND ANNA HOWARD SHAW
AS WOMANLY LEADERS

Consciousness, Commitment, and Character

To the Women Pioneers of America

They cut a path through tangled underwood
Of old traditions, out to broader ways
They lived to hear their work called brave and good,
But oh! the thorns before the crown of bays.
The world gives lashes to its Pioneers
Until the goal is reached—then deafening cheers.

Anna Howard Shaw, *The Story of a Pioneer*

Agitation for woman suffrage spanned over seventy years, officially beginning in 1848 with the Seneca Falls Convention and culminating with the passage of the Nineteenth Amendment in 1919. Anna Howard Shaw's salute to
these women pioneers speaks to the challenges that advocates for woman suffrage confronted. Initially these women struggled for the right to speak from
a public platform to a "mixed" audience. Later they faced charges that they
were "manly" women and that enfranchisement would "unsex" all women,
creating domestic chaos and social demoralization. While few suffrage supporters called for women to abandon their traditional roles entirely, they were
urging, sometimes knowingly and sometimes unknowingly, the expansion of
the realm of activities and behaviors deemed appropriate for their sex. They
were, in effect, redefining womanhood. In so doing, together with others such
as Willard and Goldman, they were creating an audience for their work.

Leaders of the woman's rights movement faced a distinctive persuasive
problem. As advocates, they became symbols of their cause. On the one hand,
in the public eye, they had to model the "new women" who could assume the
franchise while remaining loyal wives, mothers, daughters, and sisters. On the

63

other hand, they had to explain cogently the reasons they wished to move beyond those traditional familial roles. In their speeches, pamphlets, and articles they directly addressed their reasons for seeking suffrage. But two leaders of the National American Woman Suffrage Association left other records of their commitment to the cause: autobiographies written in advance of the passage of the Nineteenth Amendment. Those works by Elizabeth Cady Stanton and Anna Howard Shaw are the focus of this chapter.

The contexts in which these two women penned their life stories differ from each other and from those of the women discussed in previous chapters. Cady Stanton wrote *Eighty Years & More* (1898), as the title suggests, after many years of involvement in the woman's rights movement with no immediate hope of gaining suffrage. Moreover, the publication of *The Woman's Bible* (1895) less than three years before had generated strong criticism within the suffrage movement and had confirmed her continuing radicalism in regard to woman's rights. In writing her life story Cady Stanton realigned herself to some extent with the more conservative elements in the movement; she offered the book as "the story of my private life as the wife of an earnest reformer, as an enthusiastic housekeeper, proud of my skill in every department of domestic economy, and as the mother of seven children."[1] Although she did not disguise her views, Cady Stanton took pains to frame her narrative with details that highlighted the roles she identified.[2]

In contrast, Shaw wrote in 1915 when a resurgence of progress toward suffrage promised the long-awaited goal of a federal amendment. Moreover, never as acerbic as Cady Stanton, Shaw enjoyed wide public respect. During World War I, for example, she was asked to chair the Woman's Committee of the Council of National Defense, which coordinated women's activities in support of the war. After the war the League to Enforce the Peace asked her to be part of a group of three persons (the others were former president William Howard Taft and former president of Harvard Abbott Lawrence Lowell) that would lobby for support of the League of Nations.[3] Shaw had become, in some ways, the quintessential supporter of woman suffrage, and in her autobiography she, like Cady Stanton, is at pains to present an appealing image of the soon-to-be-enfranchised modern woman.

Unlike Willard and Goldman, however, these women faced no immediately compelling exigencies in writing their autobiographies. Although as controversial as Willard, Cady Stanton had stepped down as president of the National American Woman Suffrage Association; of advanced years, she had willingly surrendered active leadership of her cause. She was not, as was Willard, threatened with a loss of power. In addition, her longtime ally and friend Susan B. Anthony had assumed the presidency of NAWSA; the cause was, she felt, in good hands. Shaw enjoyed considerable respect; her autobiography was the record of a life dedicated to what was fast becoming a successful cause.

Both Cady Stanton and Shaw were documenting the value of their experiences as social reformers. Their dedication to their cause and their desire to demonstrate the importance of it in their lives prompted Elizabeth Cady Stanton and Anna Howard Shaw to write their life stories. William L. Howarth underscores the impact of one's work or cause for such persons: "The theme is vocation, the special summons that guided an entire life's work and now its story. Work made the story, story remakes the work: they justify each other by reducing all complexities to a single substance."[4] At the end of long careers, both Cady Stanton and Shaw sought to frame their lives as records of devotion to their cause. Contemplating their past activities with the realization that their cause had not yet won public assent, they sought to make their efforts meaningful for their followers who would continue their work. In contrast to Emma Goldman, Cady Stanton and Shaw crafted autobiographies that were rhetorically compelling on two fronts: (1) they offered a convincing depiction of their commitment as stemming from both familial background and particular experiences; and (2) they successfully modeled a "new woman" who sought an expanded sphere without sacrificing traditional values. As a result, their autobiographies, in contrast to Willard's, which relied on a personal divine commission, worked to empower other women to follow their lead.

ELIZABETH CADY STANTON AND ANNA HOWARD SHAW: DIFFERENT PATHS TO A COMMON CAUSE

Although both Cady Stanton and Shaw devoted almost their entire lives to the cause of suffrage and served as presidents of the National American Woman Suffrage Association, their personal backgrounds and roles within the movement differed significantly.[5] Elizabeth Cady, the daughter of a settled New York family, enjoyed the amenities and advantages open to the child of a successful lawyer and onetime member of Congress. She received a sound education, including her self-motivated study of Latin and Greek, and excelled in her course work. When she discovered she could not accompany her male peers to Union College at Schenectady because no girls were permitted there, she finished her education at Mrs. Willard's Seminary in Troy. Later, over her parents' objections, she married Henry B. Stanton, a prominent abolitionist. As she describes their life together: "we lived together, without more than the usual matrimonial friction, for nearly half a century, had seven children, all but one of whom is still living, and have been well sheltered, clothed, and fed, enjoying sound minds in sound bodies."[6] Her autobiography, written when she was eighty, reflects activities and involvements typical of many other middle-class women.

Cady Stanton played a distinctive role within the movement. She was one of the initiators of the 1848 Seneca Falls Convention, which signaled the beginning of the organized movement. Cady Stanton identifies herself as the source of ideas and rhetoric in her well-known alliance with Susan B. Anthony, crediting Anthony with the drive and the factual resources necessary to forge effective arguments (166). After the disappointments with the Fourteenth Amendment, which had granted black males rights denied to all women, Cady Stanton became vocally and visibly more radical. Her work with Anthony on the radical periodical *The Revolution;* their founding of the National Woman Suffrage Association with membership open only to women; and, more recently, her work on *The Woman's Bible,* which the National American Woman Suffrage Association repudiated—all placed her among the most controversial thinkers in the suffrage camp.[7]

In contrast to Cady Stanton, Anna Howard Shaw, the child of English immigrants, experienced an often harsh and limited childhood because of her father's improvident plan to homestead in Michigan. She pursued her education, most particularly her degree in theology, in defiance of her family and with no support from them. Taken together, her success as a pastor on Cape Cod, her attainment of a medical degree, and her later career as a professional public lecturer who never married marked her as quite different from most women in the audience she addressed for the suffrage movement. Her sense of her own distinctiveness led her to entitle her autobiography *The Story of a Pioneer.*

Shaw, who was younger than Cady Stanton, also played a different role in the movement. Her introduction to suffrage was through her temperance work. Never an original thinker or theorist, she worked most successfully as a public lecturer and advocate. When Cady Stanton retired from active campaigning, Shaw replaced her at Susan B. Anthony's side during the rigorous campaigns of the late nineteenth century. Her career as a lecturer did little to prepare her for administrative work, and although she served as president of the NAWSA longer than anyone, her final years in the office were beset with tensions; her tenure has been generally regarded as ineffectual.[8] Despite these facts, she showed high ethos both within and outside the movement.

Despite their differences, both Cady Stanton and Shaw agreed to write their autobiographies because of their commitment to their cause. In the preface to her work Cady Stanton avers that "the interest of my family and friends" has prompted her to relate "the story of my private life as the wife of an earnest reformer, as an enthusiastic housekeeper, proud of my skill in every department of domestic economy, and as the mother of seven children" for the amusement and benefit of readers. The details of her public life as "a leader of the most momentous reform yet launched upon the world—the emancipation of woman" are, she notes, to be found in *The History of Woman Suffrage.* However, most of her autobiography is devoted to details of her work as a suffrage advocate, and, after the initial section, her family and personal life receive little attention. Estelle C. Jelinek concludes that Cady Stanton's personal narrative was really only a "relief" for the "second, more weighty goal" of educating her readers about the suffrage movement.[9] In my view, Jelinek overlooks the rhetorical significance of Cady Stanton's personal narrative.

According to Elizabeth Jordan, who is listed as a collaborator on Shaw's autobiography because she arranged for a stenographer to transcribe Shaw's recollections and then edited them, Anna Howard Shaw agreed to record her memories only at Jordan's insistence that her life would make interesting reading. Jordan remembered that in a letter to Shaw about the project she added an argument that "I knew would strongly appeal to her—that as her life was interwoven with the woman suffrage cause the history of one would be the history of the other and must inevitably help the cause."[10]

Apparently, then, both women undertook to write their autobiographies not as purely personal explorations, but as complements to other histories of the cause to which they had devoted their lives. Both are "oratorical" autobiographies in that they concentrate on the vocation to which the women were drawn and that colored their entire lives. Moreover, both develop similar themes as they depict themselves growing gradually, almost unconsciously, into commitment to the cause of woman's rights as experiences in their lives force them to confront the unnatural, unwarranted restraints on women. Despite their desire for a greater compass for their activities as women, both remain firmly loyal to many traditional female roles and values.

NARRATIVES OF COMMITMENT: GROWING AWARENESS AND CONTINUING ENACTMENT

Because Cady Stanton and Shaw wrote their autobiographies with a clear eye to the history of the suffrage movement and their roles in it, they offer the reader a chronicle of their growing awareness of the need for reform. As they recall their lives, both trace their slow realization of the problems confronting women. This thematic thread of "emergent ideology" suggests that they derived their beliefs about women's rights inductively from their experiences in the world. Despite the disparate details of their lives, the two women depict a common pattern in their growing commitment to women's rights, which involved three phases: a gradual awareness of the tension between their intuitive sense of their own "personhood" and the socially constructed constraints of "womanhood"; a growing realization of and confidence in their own competence in overcoming the artificial and unfair limitations imposed by social stereotypes about females; and a sense that they could pursue new roles and activities without sacrificing their "womanly" values.

Both Cady Stanton and Shaw use the chronological structure of their narratives to trace the emergence of their ideology from lived experiences and their reflections on them. Using this approach, they craft narratives that pass the criterion of narrative probability as Walter R. Fisher describes it. Their stories "make sense" because they give readers accounts of the detailed experiences that produced their beliefs. Many of these experiences are poignant. In offering these details, the authors invite readers to recall events in their own lives that revealed the same patterns, problems, and pains. Because Cady Stanton and Shaw trace their lives from childhood to adult activism, readers can perceive the development and gradual formation of their characters and personalities. In short, their stories are coherent and compelling rhetorical narratives.

GRADUAL AWARENESS

Cady Stanton begins her autobiography on a philosophical note, observing that "The psychical growth of a child is not influenced by days and years, but by the impressions passing events make on its mind. What may prove a sudden awakening to one, giving an impulse in a certain direction that may last for years, may make no impression on another" (1). Embedded in her narrative of her early life are several key events and impressions that forced her to realize the demeaning and unjust stereotypes that controlled women's lives. Significantly, the first event "engraved on" her memory was the reaction to the birth of a sister, which had excited the young Elizabeth. The birth elicited the comment "What a pity it is she's a girl!" from so many family friends that she "felt a kind of compassion for the little baby. True, our family consisted of five girls and only one boy, but I did not understand at the time that girls were considered an inferior order of beings" (4). Confessing her impatience with child-rearing practices that involved "the constant cribbing and crippling of a child's life," she nonetheless recalls the happy times and pleasant memories as she grew up in a loving, if constraining, environment (11).

Her only brother's death when she was eleven was an event "which changed considerably the current of my life." Attempting to comfort her father, who was bereft by "the wreck of all his hopes in the loss of a dear son," Elizabeth was met with the response "Oh, my daughter, I wish you were a boy!" Her reaction was immediate: "Throwing my arms about his neck, I replied: 'I will try to be all my brother was'" (21). She enthusiastically threw herself into the study of Greek, which (along with the ability to manage a horse) she perceived as a key to being like a boy. Although she worked arduously, "hoping some day to hear my father say: 'Well, a girl is as good as a boy after all,'" she was repeatedly disappointed. Despite her success and pride at receiving prizes in both Latin and Greek, her father's response turned her exultation to sadness: "He kissed me on the forehead and exclaimed, with a sigh, 'Ah, you should have been a boy!'" (23).

Other, less personally traumatic episodes added to her growing awareness of socially sanctioned attitudes toward women and the injustice in them. Her father's law practice, for example, provided cases of women who suffered severe injustices because of their lack of legal rights. Cady Stanton sought to remedy that situation by cutting the offending laws from the books in her father's office; he explained the futility of that measure and counseled her when grown "to prepare a speech . . . [and] I [will] go down to Albany and talk to the legislators" (32). Later when her father and a male cousin, under the guise of protecting her, urged her against marrying Henry Stanton, she, despite her trepidation, realized that the "love of protection" often assumed by males "too often degenerates into downright tyranny" (62). In her autobiography Stanton recalls that when she saw Lucretia Coffin Mott refuse a seat as a delegate to an antislavery meeting in London in 1840, she realized dramatically how severely social stereotypes constrained women, even in their efforts to work for important causes.

Shaw's commitment to women's rights was equally gradual but different in substance. Growing up in the Michigan wilderness and confronting the "relentless limitations of pioneer life" on a daily basis, she was forced to move outside the normal realm of female activities. While her sisters and mother performed the usual female work of cooking, cleaning, and sewing, Shaw and her brothers did the outside work, even digging a well to provide water. Her first recognition of the problems women faced came through her mother's experiences. Confronted with the rude cabin her husband had prepared for the family in the Michigan wilderness, Shaw's mother gave way to despair. Shaw recalls that as her father worked and enjoyed the stimulation of life in Massachusetts, he sent the family money as he was able and "a generous supply of improving literature for our minds. It remained for us to strengthen our bodies to meet the conditions in which he had placed us and to survive if we could."[11] Later in the autobiography, discussing her father's personality, Shaw to some extent excuses his insensitivity, tracing it to his idealism; but she adds:

> Like most men, my dear father should never have married. . . . In practical matters he remained to the end of his days as irresponsible as a child. Even if he had witnessed my mother's despair on the night of our arrival in our new home, he would not have understood it. From his viewpoint, he was doing a man's duty. He was working steadily in Lawrence, and, incidentally, giving much time to the Abolition cause and to other big public movements of his day which had his interest and sympathy. (28–29)

Shaw first personally confronted the barriers to women when she decided to pursue her education and work to become a minister. When she preached publicly for the first time, her family was horrified. Her brother-in-law inserted in a local newspaper a notice that expressed the family's reaction: "A young girl named Anna Shaw . . . preached at Ashton yesterday. Her real friends deprecate the course she is pursuing" (62). Although other persons encouraged her in these efforts, her family remained adamant against her, and a painful estrangement began. The attitude toward women of at least one male in her school—he opined that they could not manage meetings on their own—incensed Shaw and led her to join an all-female club rather than the coeducational one the man had proposed. However, she soon recognized that "whenever there was an advantage of any kind to be secured the men invariably got it." This led her to organize her first protest for women's rights (71).

Theology school provided far more bitter lessons. The sole woman in her class at Boston University, Shaw faced almost insurmountable financial hardships because of blatant sexual discrimination. Unlike the males, who received room and board in a dormitory for $1.25, Shaw reports: "For me no such kindly provision was made. I was not allowed a place in the dormitory, but instead given two dollars a week to pay the rent of a room outside. Neither was I admitted to the economical comforts of the club, but fed myself according to my income, which worked admirably when there was an income, but left an obvious void when there was not" (83).

Predictably, males received most of the opportunities to earn extra money by preaching. Thus, Shaw was nearly destitute and often hungry (83–84). These difficulties were compounded by the prejudices she confronted in class. Admitting that she felt keenly her isolation as the only woman in the class, Shaw concludes: "Naturally, I missed a great deal of class fellowship and class support, and throughout my entire course I rarely entered my class-room without the abysmal conviction I was not really wanted there" (93).

Although Cady Stanton was considerably more introspective than Shaw, and although their experiences differ sharply, both depict quite effectively the process that led them to their commitment to work for women's rights. The focus in their narratives is on how experiences and events shaped their perceptions. In both cases their feminist ideology emerged primarily from their personal confrontations with the constraints and stereotypes imposed by societal ideas of womanhood. Because the autobiographies depict concretely how both women came to recognize the need for a change, they seem demonstrative cases rather than didactic arguments.

CONFIDENT AND COMPETENT . . . BUT STILL WOMEN

A sense of the injustices toward women and of the problems they confronted could not assure commitment to working toward change. Also required was a confidence in one's ability to meet challenges and accomplish tasks. Both Cady Stanton and Shaw used their narratives to demonstrate how women could behave competently and efficiently in various situations; in each case their hard-won self-confidence stemmed, at least in part, from their educational and academic successes. Still, on other levels their paths to such self-confidence differed markedly.

The section of Cady Stanton's autobiography that treats her early married life, especially the birth of her first child, is particularly significant in this respect. Her unusually detailed account of the early care of the infant contrasts sharply with her meager attention to motherhood thereafter.[12] What is significant about her narration here is the attention she pays to her competence and wisdom as a parent who relies on common sense and evidence in contrast to the trained professional (in)competence of the nurse and male physicians. Avowing that motherhood is the most important of professions, she deplores women's lack of preparation for it. Rejecting traditional practices and procedures, she read extensively on the topic but was wary, because of Angelina Grimké Weld's experience, of relying too heavily even on "scientific" writing.[13] She chose to rely on her own good sense and what she deemed to be the sound advice of one author. In defiance of the nurse, she refused to "bandage" the child, as was the custom, and insisted on plenty of fresh air. When the physician's treatment of the child's misaligned collar bone seemed counterproductive, Cady Stanton pursued her own practical remedy. It worked beautifully.

These experiences, she noted, taught her an important lesson in self-reliance. "I trusted neither men nor books absolutely after this, either in regard to heavens above or the earth beneath." She strongly urged every woman to use her "'mother's instinct,' if 'reason' is too dignified a term to apply to woman's thoughts." Cady Stanton records how she shared her experiences with young parents during her lecture tours, often producing remarkable results with unhappy infants (120–26).

In the same section she relates her skill, pride, and satisfaction in her domestic life. At first she enjoyed the control she exercised within her home, taking great satisfaction in her domestic economy. Using "the most approved cook books," she spent "half my time preserving, pickling, and experimenting in new dishes." Her drive to excel communicated itself to her laundress, who soon sought to have the whitest clothes out earliest to dry and ironed and stored most rapidly. She reveled in cleanliness and order. Of these years she recalls, "I put my soul into everything, and hence enjoyed it. . . . I spent some of the happiest days of my life, enjoying, in turn, the beautiful outlook, my children, and my books" (136, 138).

Without doubting the sincerity of her sentiments, the reader can clearly perceive Cady Stanton's affirmation of the roles and values associated with womanhood. Enjoyment and perfection of these "womanly" arts mark her life at this point. But at the same time, she relishes her books and the stimulating environment around Boston. The move to Seneca Falls disrupts her rapture and makes her more fully aware of the plight of most women. The increasing weight of domestic responsibilities with the birth of more children and her inability to hire good help, the social isolation, and the ebbing novelty of the challenges of domestic life took their toll. She remembers vividly:

> I now fully understood the practical difficulties most women had to contend with in the isolated household, and the impossibility of woman's best development if in contact, the chief part of her life, with servants and children. . . . The general discontent I felt with woman's portion as wife, mother, housekeeper, physician, and spiritual guide, the chaotic conditions into which everything fell without her constant supervision, and the wearied, anxious look of the majority of women impressed me with a strong feeling that some active measures should be taken to remedy the wrongs of society in general, and of women in particular. (148)

These sentiments underlay her decision to call the Seneca Falls Convention, which she saw as a way to effect change. At this point in her narrative, her focus shifts to her activities in service to the cause, eclipsing any substantial treatment of her personal life. Notably, however, Cady Stanton did not repudiate the traditional roles open to women; rather she traces her own enjoyment of them before concluding that such roles were simply insufficient and too constraining for her continued happiness and fulfillment. Experience had confirmed the joys of traditional roles but had also taught her the unfair constrictions on women. Moreover, her experiences had convinced her of her own competence in handling problems.

In Shaw's case, confidence in her own abilities and a freedom from normal restraints to some extent preceded her awareness of the limitations of womanhood. Her unusual familial responsibilities early in life, her father's apparent improvidence in providing for the family, and the rigors of coping with pioneer life all bred early confidence in her own competence. Like Cady Stanton, she enjoyed substantial academic success, and her perseverance at theology school, despite financial and personal hardships, hardened her resolve. Although she admits that she doubted her calling when faced with such hardships, her ultimate triumph over them undoubtedly fueled her feeling that she was pursuing her God-given destiny. Success in dealing with her Cape Cod congregation, both in overcoming their initial prejudices against her and in exerting a firm pastoral hand, confirmed her self-confidence.

Despite the fact that she did not lead a conventional family life, in various ways Shaw clearly reveals her commitment to the values and ideals of womanhood. She repeatedly mentions her family and especially her joy at ending the familial estrangement produced by her pursuit of a degree in theology. A dutiful daughter, she subsidized her parents in their old age. She writes, "I had the privilege, a very precious one, of seeing they were well cared for and contented." When her sister died, she wanted her nieces and nephews to live with her but realized they were better off with her parents (140). She also recalls obtaining for her mother a bunch of real English heather, "a trifle which gave her a pleasure out of all proportion to what I had dreamed it would do" (178).

Although she mentions no romances with men, she does report her desire to have a child and her attempt, at one point, to adopt a neglected child from his drunken mother. She managed to take the child home with her briefly and provided him with new clothes. Of this brief period she writes, "every hour I had him tightened his hold on my heart-strings." Despite entreaties, however, the mother refused to let her have the child and even sold the new clothes to buy drink. For her own peace of mind, Shaw relates, she abandoned the efforts to gain custody; but she adds, "I have never ceased to regret the little adopted son I might have had" (144).[14]

In addition to her affirmation of family values and her own pleasure in her role as caretaker, Shaw also expresses her love of home. One entire chapter of her autobiography is devoted to her building of a home. In part, she admits, she was prompted to build her own dwelling because she had acquired an array of furniture at the auctions she enjoyed attending. But she also argues, "I have always longed for a home." Later she contends, "Every suffragist I have ever met has been a lover of home; and only the conviction that she is fighting for her home, her children, for other women, or for all of these, has sustained her public work" (264, 269). She recalls that in the midst of a gala celebration in Oregon, after being driven through the streets and crowned with a laurel wreath, "if ever a women felt that her place was in the home and longed to be in her place, I felt it that day" (270). Such sentiments and the pictures of her home included among the few photographs in her book clearly convey her appreciation for this key value associated with womanhood.

Throughout the book Shaw also gives attention to such "womanly" concerns as the fabric of her gowns on particular occasions; the cleanliness of her accommodations; and her close, caring friendships, especially with "Aunt Susan" B. Anthony. While none of these is particularly significant by itself, together they help build an image of Shaw as a "womanly" woman despite her unorthodox life.

While the narratives of Cady Stanton and Shaw differ in many respects, the themes of confidence, competence, and womanliness emerge in quite similar ways in their stories. In both cases the women use the chronological structure typical of autobiography to show their gradual development as persons before they become social activists in their adulthood. Their ability to overcome obstacles and their awareness of the problems of their gender frame the balance of their lives as activists. The theme of womanliness dominates the initial section of Cady Stanton's book, where she details her early years of marriage and raising a family. For Shaw, the memories of her childhood in the early chapters reveal a great regard for her mother and grandmother, both strong women who became her role models in some respects. The themes of womanliness and love of home persist throughout the work. In both books the women establish themselves as competent, confident women before they chronicle their involvement in the cause of woman suffrage.

CRAFTING A PUBLIC PERSONA: STRATEGIC ADAPTATION TO AN AUDIENCE

Rhetorically, Cady Stanton and Shaw employ two broad, distinctive persuasive strategies in their narratives. First, they depict their commitment to woman's rights as emerging from real-life experiences. They had come to believe the doctrine of woman's rights because the world had shown them the need for changes in the status of females. Significantly, the incidents which they record as contributing to their growing awareness are touching human episodes, painful to the empathetic reader. Rather than arguing directly and explicitly about the need for suffrage, Cady Stanton and Shaw depict how they have discovered the reasons for such action in their own lives. This indirect argument from real experience is more concrete and potentially more affecting than rigorous and traditional forms of evidence and reasoning.

Moreover, significantly in both cases, the consciousness-producing episodes are depicted as arising from their efforts to live up to values that were central in their society, although perhaps not usually associated with women. In Cady Stanton's case, she simply sought to soothe her father's grief at the loss of a son; Shaw strove to obtain an education to serve her religious calling. Their recollections of the sources of their motivation make the prejudices the women confronted more objectionable. Because of the nature of autobiography, these crucial episodes are embedded in other memories and events, many of which reveal happy times in childhood and early life. Both the context of the experiences and their location in youth add force to the depictions. The reader identifies with the enthusiasms and dreams of youth and enjoys the happier moments with the writers, while being shown subtly the problems that confronted them both.

Second, Cady Stanton and Shaw, as leaders of the woman's movement, enact its tenets. They are, by implication, the type of woman the movement seeks to produce. Their commitments are strong, their beliefs clear; both have emerged from their experiences to form the guiding principles of their lives. While rhetors can enact an ideology or argument within a single speech, each of these longer works offers an even greater opportunity to demonstrate the impact of an ideology on a life. Cady Stanton's and Shaw's lives are notable because of their commitment to the cause of suffrage; but, on the other hand, that commitment stamped their lives and personalities. Their enactment of their beliefs, narrated in their autobiographies, is compelling "proof" of the healthy influence of their doctrines.

While these works reveal the natural course of consciousness-raising within the lives of these two women, they also suggest how Cady Stanton and Shaw have been able to convey images of themselves as significant persons and as women who reflect many of the cultural values associated with that role. Without abandoning allegiance to many interests and values associated with traditional women's roles, these two implicitly argue for the opening up of new opportunities and larger vistas for females. Their lives serve as models for how women can both retain their femininity and assert their worthiness as persons. Cady Stanton and Shaw represent the "new women" who incorporate the best of the old and the promise of the new.[15]

These two strategies were particularly well suited for the audiences that Cady Stanton and Shaw addressed. Eleanor Flexner argues convincingly that various social factors, among them an increasing polarization of social classes in the last part of the nineteenth century, led the suffrage movement "into the camp of decorum." As a result, the leadership and membership of the suffrage association were increasingly drawn from professional and middle-class women, who were not sympathetic to demands for radical change. Particularly after the so-called "divorce debate" of 1860, the woman's rights movement drifted steadily toward "the conservative and the conventional."[16]

For such a constituency Cady Stanton's and Shaw's depictions and narrations of the model of a "new woman" offered dual appeals. On the one hand, because they did not reject outright the tenets of "true womanhood" or repudiate the values associated with that stereotype, they offered their readers a comfortable security. Rather than asking women to abandon the socially constructed gender roles to which they had been acculturated, Cady Stanton and Shaw offered a superficially easier alternative: women could retain many of their values and work within the system, as its moral guardians, to purify the existing order. Following the models of Cady Stanton and Shaw, they could work for socially constructive causes, in particular women's rights, without abandoning their allegiance to home and family. The *New York Times* reviewer wrote of Cady Stanton's book: "An earnest reformer was she, but the volume shows the delight she felt in being an excellent housekeeper and, how, as the mother of a large family, she cared for her children. Mrs. Cady Stanton has shown that some women can advance the social conditions of their own sex and yet be good wives and mothers."[17]

These stories reflect the fidelity Fisher sees as crucial to compelling rhetorical narratives. For supporters of woman's rights their stories embody values that the cause prizes: competence, confidence, and good sense. For other readers their allegiance to home and family are appealing. For both kinds of readers these narratives project images of women that are attractive and achievable; their lives are reasonable models for women who wish to be socially responsible persons in a changing world.

In their autobiographies both women are careful to reveal themselves as "ordinary" women, resisting the temptation to construct daunting personal mythologies. Cady Stanton's intertwining of personal details with her professional activism makes her perspective and life seem less radical than they in fact were. Jelinek notes that, in highlighting her "ordinariness," Cady Stanton creates a persona in her autobiography that is often inconsistent with her public role.[18] Her ordinariness is, in fact, a carefully crafted rhetorical strategy:

> Cady Stanton's intention as stated in her preface—to write about her "private life" as opposed to her "public career"—does not exactly give us the whole picture. . . . The account of her private life as wife-housekeeper-mother is not given enough coverage in *Eighty Years* for us to believe Cady Stanton's assertion. . . . Cady Stanton's actual intention is twofold. She wants to present herself as an ordinary human being, but *not* as a wife-housekeeper-mother. She is ordinary because she mixes easily with ordinary people, has a cheerful disposition, is self-reliant and healthy, and has varied domestic interests in addition to her political ones. This ordinary person plays an important role in the anecdotes she relates to relieve the narrative of its more weighty and actual though unstated goal: to educate her readers about the women's suffrage movement in order to convert them to her cause.[19]

Although less controversial in her expressed views than Cady Stanton, Shaw deviated from proscribed roles in her professional life: she was an ordained minister as well as a physician; she was a woman who supported herself almost entirely by public lecturing; she was a single woman, living with a close female companion, in an age that saw marriage and family as central to women's identities. But as we have seen, Shaw goes out of her way in her autobiography to depict herself as a home-loving woman who longs for the children and family life she has sacrificed for the cause.

Thus, both works effectively negotiate the tension between the tendency toward personal mythologizing typical of many autobiographies and the imitability essential for authors wishing to attract converts to a cause. The inconsistency that Jelinek notes in Cady Stanton's *Eighty Years* between the "ordinary" woman and the forceful public advocate reflects her efforts to construct both a memorable and an imitable public persona. For both Shaw and Cady Stanton the tensions between personal mythology and imitability were exacerbated by gender issues. While critical readers such as Jelinek may perceive the resultant inconsistencies, sympathetic readers can easily overlook them. In a sense, the inconsistencies Jelinek reveals in Cady Stanton's account and those we have explored in the works of both women are evidence of their strategic adaptation in the face of a difficult rhetorical challenge.

In addition to offering readers a comfortable, imitable approach to womanhood, these books also empowered them. By depicting the problems women faced (especially in Shaw's case) and how they were able to surmount them, the works showed readers that they too could be competent and resourceful. Because a reader can identify with the personal frustrations of each woman, she can also exult in and relish the successes. That the two women overcame difficulties and became prominent, respected public figures suggested the possibilities open to persistent women. In fact, the acts of writing the autobiographies were themselves proof of the status and success of the authors.

The contribution of Cady Stanton's and Shaw's autobiographies was, in part, to provide a nonthreatening, even attractive image of the new woman a reader might become. This image was concrete, developed through the relating of real personal experiences; it was a valuable complement to their formal arguments for the cause and a suggestive example of the potential of the new woman. Through their autobiographies Cady Stanton and Shaw provided persuasive role models for their readers.

Undoubtedly, Karlyn Kohrs Campbell is accurate in arguing that the early movement's failure to resolve the tensions between personhood and womanhood necessitated another feminist initiative. But while the attempt to emphasize womanhood rather than personhood was unsatisfactory in addressing the broad range of feminist issues, it was not a rhetorical mistake. If the audience for Shaw's and Cady Stanton's books was largely middle-class and relatively conservative, the radical feminist position (which Cady Stanton had long espoused in other forums) may not have been rhetorically wise. Cady Stanton and Shaw were forced to operate in a particular social and cultural milieu; their rhetorical choices were not unconstrained. Their choice of depicting the possibility of a "new woman" who embraced the best of the old and the promise of the new was an expedient and successful ploy for the early woman's movement. In Cady Stanton's case, it attracted and reinforced the type of audience that was necessary to move and keep the woman's movement in the acceptable mainstream of political activity. While the movement lost the involvement of some groups, such as immigrants and workers, it cemented the support of women who had the time and money to sustain a long campaign. Shaw, in the face of the more confrontational methods of the young suffragettes, was able to maintain an association that appealed to more conservative women. Certainly the efforts of Alice Paul and Harriot Stanton Blatch enlivened interest in suffrage and impelled political action, but the middle-class women to whom Shaw's depiction appealed were still an impor-

tant constituency in the push for the Nineteenth Amendment. Thus, the appeal
to the possibility of a "new woman" was rhetorically shrewd, even if it did not
embrace an expansive feminist ideology.

While this approach did not resolve the tension inherent in feminist ideology, it probably did facilitate passage of the Nineteenth Amendment. The
amendment was not a panacea. Many of its supporters realized its limitations.
But it was symbolically and practically important for women. Not only did it
confer real political power and status, but it also suggested that when women
joined together they could achieve significant victories. Whether this success
could have been achieved without ideological compromise is uncertain, but its
importance for women is clear.

RHETORICAL POTENTIALS OF AUTOBIOGRAPHIES

While the books of Cady Stanton and Shaw were clearly significant for the
nineteenth-century woman's movement, this case study highlights some
rhetorical potentials of autobiographies as a genre. These potentials derive
from the reader's expectations for the autobiographical form and the bond that
can unite author and reader.

In considering the nature of autobiography, Barrett J. Mandel asserts: "It is
simply a fact that readers turn to autobiography for the kind of satisfaction that
one derives from reading something true rather than fabular. . . . The autobiography [as genre] embodies truth when the reader seeks confirmation of his
or her own perceptions of reality in terms of those experienced by another mortal. . . . Readers turn to autobiography to satisfy a need for verifying a fellow
human being's experience of reality."[20] James Olney is more succinct: "What
one seeks in reading autobiography is not a date, a name, or a place, but a characteristic way of perceiving, of organizing, and of understanding, an individual way of feeling and expressing that one can somehow relate to oneself."[21]

The act of reading these works forges a distinctive kind of bond between
the author/rhetor and the reader. Reading is an individual experience; the
author speaks directly to one. What results, in one sense, is a kind of interpersonal communication and consciousness sharing; the reader forms a personal bond with the author. Of course, this relationship need not always be
positive; some people choose to read works by authors they find objectionable
or unattractive. Since, through the process of selective perception, such readers are probably immune to the appeal of the narratives, such cases are not
relevant here. But for readers open to the messages of an autobiography, the
intimate experience of reading and the narrator's voice may produce a kind of
personal relationship difficult to duplicate through public meetings or other
printed matter. Moreover, the authorial voice in autobiography carries unusual
weight and impact. Because such works are usually written at the end of long

public careers (as Cady Stanton's and Shaw's were), the reader expects to gain insights and perhaps wisdom from the author. While some orators enjoy or build high ethos with particular audiences, readers of autobiographies anticipate that age will enable the author to share the benefits of her/his experiences. The act of writing an autobiography, the reader assumes, requires reflection and self-analysis. We expect the author to share the benefits of that introspection with us. An author's satisfaction with her life as lived provides a powerful argument for the value and significance of the principles that have governed her choices. For example, Cady Stanton and Shaw both avow strongly that their commitment to woman's rights has given meaning and richness to their lives. Such assertions, following their recital of the problems and difficulties they have faced, ennoble the cause they espouse.

These features allow autobiographical narratives to supplement and complement formal arguments rhetorically in several important ways. Because the implicit arguments for a cause are made indirectly through the relating of personal experiences, the reader participates in their construction. The intimacy between author and reader inherent in autobiography encourages belief and acceptance of the truth of the experiences related. By comparing one's own experiences to those recalled by the author, one tests the truth, or in Walter Fisher's terms the fidelity, of the narrative within one's own life. Albert E. Stone observes: "Reading another's life story is . . . to immerse oneself in human experience in all its interconnections and manifestations. . . . Readers . . . derive a deep satisfaction from sharing the act of memory and imagination which connects a self to the 'extensive totality' of the world."[22] While concrete personal examples in formal arguments may work in a similar fashion, the differing contexts are significant. Examples in public presentations are offered to support claims and to advance arguments. They invite questioning and even refutation. In contrast, examples embedded in a narrative frame are part of a larger, more complex, and gradually unfolding story. They do not admit direct refutation, but they do invite empathy and understanding.

In oratorical autobiographies the narrative structure permits the authors to utilize what might be called refutation through demonstration. For example, among other things, opponents of woman suffrage frequently alleged that the ballot would "unsex" women and destroy the family. The hypothetical repercussions were often coupled with personal slurs on the leaders as fanatics and termagants. Moreover, opponents, even women themselves, often contended that females could not handle the responsibility of the ballot. Suffragists, of course, refuted these charges; indeed, Shaw was well known for her humorous if biting rebuttals. But autobiography offered another alternative for response. Rather than dealing in abstractions and hypothetical cases, Shaw and Cady Stanton were able to offer their lives, as depicted in their autobiographies, as concrete case studies of the impact of woman's rights thinking on its proponents. Their lives affirmed an alternative possibility to the repercussions their opponents could only hypothesize. The evidence provided in their autobiographies did not supplant more formal arguments, but it provided an enactment of the cause they advocated. This form of refutation gains strength from the nature of the autobiographical narrative. The motives of most readers in seeking out the autobiography—the desire to confirm one experience in the life of another and to find a model for attitudes and behavior—added great force to this appeal.[23]

The depiction in an autobiography of an emergent ideology suggested the intuitive truth of the ideas. For example, Shaw's and Cady Stanton's apparently innate sense of themselves as personally worthy, evinced quite early in their lives, suggested that such awareness was integral to human consciousness. Their frustrating experiences with the strictures of womanhood offended their basic sense of their own humanity. In this sense their experiences implied that a higher truth and more basic principle underlay their arguments for woman's rights. Again, while formal argument could convey this point, what we see in these narratives is the cumulative process that produces the conviction. Formal argument begins with the product of one's thinking; it may even recite the events that produced one's conclusions. But within autobiographical narratives the reader participates in the process that yields the insight.

Readers are not, however, simple dupes in this process. Rather, as Fisher notes, they test the narrative for coherence and fidelity.[24] They may even be, as one scholar contends, quick to discover the unauthentic voice or the "unreasonable" reaction to events. Still, as they invest faith in the author, they are led to accept her reactions and interpretations as reasonable or at least understandable. Initially presumption lies with the author, who alone records her responses. As a consequence, the "good reasons" subtly offered by the author for her views may compel belief almost without the reader's consent.

Such "good reasons" become particularly forceful if the author shares with the reader her thoughts when confronted with critical episodes. For example, Cady Stanton's recalling her naive, even pitiful attempt to be like a boy to please her father and his response to her efforts lets us glimpse her first confrontation with the prejudices of her day. Similarly, her plan to cut offensive passages from law books as a remedy for the legal problems of women evinces another strategy to cope with the ills she perceived. The relating of those stories lets us see Cady Stanton testing the fidelity of the stories her society offered about women and their appropriate roles. As she rejects those stories as false and harmful, we follow her lead. Thus, within autobiographies, authors are able to test for the reader some of the alternate stories competing for their allegiance. The personal experience of the author becomes refutation of those alternate stories. Of course, the readers may well question the author's interpretations, but they are at least stimulated to confront another human's perceptions of the "truth."

As in the case of Emma Goldman, not all authors are able to draw on the rhetorical resources of the autobiographical form effectively. That Cady Stanton and Shaw were at least moderately successful in tapping the genre's potentials is further evidence of their rhetorical adroitness. As seasoned public advocates, completely dedicated to what they saw as an achievable social change, they crafted their autobiographical personae to suggest the consciousness, commitment, and character, as well as the personal values, that could distinguish the new, enfranchised woman.

CHAPTER 6

MARY CHURCH TERRELL AS
A COLORED WOMAN IN A WHITE WORLD
Demonstration and Evidence in Autobiography

This is the story of a colored woman living in a white world.
It cannot possibly be like a story written by a white woman.
A white woman has only one handicap to overcome—that of sex.
I have two—both sex and race. I belong to the only group in
this country which has two such huge obstacles to surmount.
Colored men have only one—that of race.

Mary Church Terrell, *A Colored Woman in a White World*

This opening observation in Mary Church Terrell's autobiography, *A Colored Woman in a White World,* signals a dominant theme in the work. Church Terrell, in relating her own life, demonstrates the constraints that her race and her gender have placed on her development. Published in 1940, the work reveals the ubiquity, injustice, and irrationality of racial stereotypes. More important, Church Terrell uses her life story to refute racial stereotypes, to suggest the potential of her race, and to indicate how members of her race, especially women, can have meaningful, useful lives despite the obstacles they confront.

In a sense, each of the autobiographies studied in this work use the lives of women as evidence of a social problem. Certainly, Cady Stanton and Shaw depict the obstacles they confronted as women. Goldman's repeated difficulties with authorities confirm the oppressive nature of the institutions that she deplores. However, Church Terrell's book provides the clearest example of how an author can use her life story didactically. Recalling events in her life, she repeatedly teaches the reader about racism in American society.

Church Terrell's attempts to bring the book to print confirm the obstacles she mentions. Despite her prominence in the Black community, her political connections in Washington, and her long history of social activism, the book was published by a small company in Washington, D.C., only in 1940, after several rejections by more established presses.[1] The short, positive review in the *Christian Century,* listed simply under "Books Received" rather than even the secondary-level reviews included in "Books in Brief," indicates the value of the book for Americans as a whole:

"The first full length autobiography of a colored woman."[2] It is a notable story of a notable life. It began with a rather unusual childhood for a Negro girl in the south and led through education at Oberlin and marriage to a Negro who became a judge in the District of Columbia (appointed by Theodore Roosevelt, reappointed by Taft, Wilson and Harding), to a conspicuous and useful career of her own. It is written without bitterness, but with keen awareness of the difficulties to be faced by a Negro in the white world. Such a book helps white Americans to be humble in their pride and to know their country better. H. G. Wells writes the preface.[3]

Although the review gives more attention to her husband's career than to Church Terrell's own "conspicuous and useful" activities, it is sympathetic to her work and struggles, as are the other reviews found in her personal papers. The preface by H. G. Wells, who broke his own "obstinate refusal" to write such remarks, locates Church Terrell's work explicitly in the nexus of the racial conflict in the United States.

When, as my reward for this Introduction, I get the book nicely printed and inscribed, I shall put it on my shelves not among the masterpieces of art, but as the living Mary Church Terrell, the most subtle, almost inadvertent, rendering of the stresses and views and impulses that characterise the race conflict as it appears in America. I might almost say the human conflict. . . . Mrs. Church Terrell has lived her life through a storm of burning injustices; but if she had been born a sensitive and impressionable white girl in a village on some English estate, destined normally to be an under-housemaid and marry an under-gardener, she would have had almost the same story to tell, if not in flamboyant colors then in aquatint. She would have struggled to independence and self-respect against handicaps less obvious but more insidious. She would have discovered parallel frustrations. She would have found her brothers and cousins barred, very effectively if not quite so emphatically, from education and opportunity.[4]

Although Wells clearly has his own broader political agenda, he goes on to challenge American readers to "turn over the pages of this plucky, distressful woman's naive story of the broadening streak of violence, insult, and injustice in your country, through which she has been compelled to live her life" as they contemplate the United States's struggle to attain its ideals.

Throughout the work Church Terrell acknowledges the resistance and prejudice she has confronted; thus, the absence of an enthusiastic reception would probably not surprise her. Indeed, her persistence in seeking a publisher reflects a theme of her work: her determination to accomplish her goals, despite all obstacles. Apparently a working title for her book had reflected this same theme: "A Mighty Rocky Road."[5] In outlining her goals in her "Introduction," Church Terrell insists:

> I have recorded what I have been able to accomplish in spite of the obstacles which I have had to surmount. I have done this, not because I want to tell the world how smart I am, but because both a sense of justice and a regard for truth prompt me to show what a colored woman can achieve in spite of the difficulties by which race prejudice blocks her path if she fits herself to do a certain thing, works with all her might and main to do it and is given a chance. (n.p.)

She returns to this theme at the end of the work as she reflects on the course of her life:

> So far as possible, I have tried to forget the limitations imposed upon me on account of my race and have gone ahead striving to accomplish what I wanted to do. . . . While I am grateful for the blessings which have been bestowed upon me and for the opportunities which have been offered, I cannot help wondering sometimes what I might have become and might have done if I had lived in a county which had not circumscribed and handicapped me on account of my race, but had allowed me to reach any height I was able to attain. (427)

Church Terrell's own account suggests that she intended her book to address directly the racism in American society; the responses of the anonymous reviewer and H. G. Wells indicate that her message was clearly communicated. Church Terrell offered her life both as evidence of the persistent ubiquity of racism in this country and as a demonstration of how an individual could respond creatively and constructively to that racism. In essence, her autobiography provides concrete evidence against prevalent racial stereotypes, provides a model for coping with racism, and suggests the thwarted potential of her race.

Her life was, by any reasonable standard, remarkably successful. Not only did she have a full and apparently happy personal life, but she also made significant contributions to the advancement of her race. Her involvement extended until the end of her life. In the 1950s, well into her eighties, Church Terrell was an organizer and active participant in efforts, including picketing, to force an end to segregated facilities in Washington, D.C.[6] Her narrative is, in large part, an explanation of how she was able to achieve such success, given the obstacles she faced because of her race and her gender.

Church Terrell depicts her life against the backdrop of the racism prevalent in American society. That racism constrains her achievements. Her narrative, however, provides a distinctive angle of vision on how one should and can cope with racism. In general, she eschews the sweeping condemnations of many of her contemporaries who saw the causes of racism as irremediably embedded in the American political and social institutions. Rather she saw its sources as residing in individuals, whose attitudes and outlooks could be changed. In her recollections she offers a moderate analysis of the problem of racism that suggests it is ameliorable through constructive action within the reach of most members of her race. Only Church Terrell's special advantages and privileges allowed her personally to move beyond the constraints racism placed upon most members of her race. In tandem, the prevalent racism in America and Church Terrell's own privileged position generated a keen sense of social responsibility in her. But her gender produced still other obstacles for her in fulfilling her social obligations.

Church Terrell's autobiography is largely straightforward. Primarily chronological, the narrative traces what she perceived as the significant episodes in her life with brief reflections on her reactions, thoughts, and feelings to particular events. Rhetorically, however, the work is more subtle. She intertwines discussions of racism, her own distinctive background, and her personal struggles to combine her sense of commitment to the advancement of her race with her roles as daughter, wife, and mother. Working together, these persistent motifs make the account of her life function on three levels to address the issues of racism and gender: (1) her successes demonstrate her views about the potentials of her race, refuting social stereotypes; (2) her successes indicate how others of her race can work to subvert the force of racism in their lives; and (3) her life provides a model for other affluent African American women on how to balance social responsibilities and their roles as women. Before considering the rhetorical functions of her narrative, however, let us look at how she depicts her life in dealing with the color line, in equipping herself for a life of service, and in balancing her social commitments with her roles as a woman.

LIVING WITH THE COLOR LINE

After a period of study abroad when she had completed her college education, Church Terrell returned to the United States with some trepidation. Despite her love for her native country and her determination to remain patriotic, she was realistic about the circumstances that would confront her.

> But now the time had come for me to return to my native land, and my heart ached when I thought about it. Life had been so pleasant and profitable abroad, where I could take advantage of any opportunity I desired without wondering whether a colored girl would be allowed to enjoy it or not, and where I could secure accommodations in any hotel, boarding house, or private home where I cared to live. I knew that when I

returned home I would face again the humiliations, discriminations, and hardships to which colored people are subjected all over the United States. (98)

Church Terrell's prediction derived from her own experiences. Her first experience of the "Race Problem" occurred when she was a small child, traveling north by train with her father. Since Tennessee had not yet passed Jim Crow laws, her father placed her in a "white" coach, where most "self-respecting colored people" went to avoid the dirty car set aside for them, while he went to the smoker. Clearly, such intermingling of "respectable" members of both races, which was to become anathema under Jim Crow, was still possible at this time. Soon an angry conductor, demanding to know "Whose little nigger is this?," jerked her from her seat and was prepared to take her forcibly to the "colored car." When a White friend alerted her father, a scene ensued "which no one who saw it could ever forget" (16). She sought an explanation for this incident from her father, who refused to discuss it. To her mother, who questioned her behavior, she insisted that she had been "a little lady" in every respect. Her mother's counsel may have helped shape Church Terrell's response to later racist experiences: "She explained the incident by telling me that sometimes conductors on railroad trains were unkind and treated good little girls very badly" (16).

Such a moderate response, which did not target all Whites as accomplices in racism, became a typical pattern of reaction for Church Terrell. Always she saw individuals rather than the whole White race as responsible for the injuries she endured. Her responses varied from retorts to refusal to confrontation. But at every point she retained her sense of dignity and self-worth. During her years at the Model School (which was affiliated with Antioch), for example, on one occasion a group of girls, reveling in their real and imagined beauty, answered Church Terrell's question "Haven't I got a pretty face too?" with the comment "You've got a pretty black face," accompanied by laughter and finger pointing. She was stunned into momentary silence before she managed to retort: "I don't want my face to be white like yours and look like milk. I want it nice and dark just like it is" (22–23). Later she was invited to participate in a play, to "take the part of a Negro servant who made a monkey of himself and murdered the king's English" (22). Without consulting anyone, she firmly rejected the invitation, although she was hurt and embarrassed by the obvious racism.

Even at Oberlin, which she regarded as a paradigm for congenial relationships about the races, she confronted slights and discrimination. When her Greek professor asked her to read and translate a passage for the benefit of Matthew Arnold, who was visiting the school, "Mr. Arnold expressed the greatest surprise imaginable because, he said, he thought the tongue of the

86

African was so thick he could not be taught to pronounce Greek correctly" (41). This story is embedded, however, in her fond reminiscences of her Greek professor, who later became president of Berea College.

On another occasion, because of her acknowledged skills, she was nominated as class poet, a position that would entail being a speaker at the Junior Exhibition. To counter her nomination, one classmate offered the name of a young man who "had never written a poem in his life, so far as the class had heard, and had never exhibited any talent in that direction, so far as the class knew" (43). After several ballots she wished to withdraw her name, but friends prevented her from doing so. Finally, he was elected. Although she avers that she was probably justified in seeing the development as reflecting racial prejudice, she sees the entire episode in a balanced light:

> But I did not allow this episode to embitter me at all. On the contrary, it encouraged and comforted me greatly to see how many of my class-mates stood by me so long. I knew also that they finally voted for the young man, so as to break the deadlock, after they saw that a few of his friends were determined to elect him. There is no doubt whatever that on this one occasion at least, the fact that I am a colored prevented me from receiving the honor which many members of my class thought my record proved I deserved. (43)

Later her college confers other honors on her, often seeking her out with invitations. Despite her justifiable disappointment on the occasion mentioned earlier, she concludes: "I feel I have little reason to complain about discrimination on account of race while I was a student in Oberlin College" (45).

Seeking temporary employment while staying with her mother in New York during her summer vacation from college, Church Terrell had her "first bitter experience of inability to secure employment on account of my race." In three interviews women told her that she "possessed just the qualities they desired and were very complimentary indeed," but no offers ensued. At the end of another, the woman asked her about her race and, after professing that she had "no prejudice against colored people herself, she said, her servants were white and she was certain they would leave if she employed a colored girl." On still another occasion she was offered a position, only to receive a letter later asking about her race. Her candid response brought a cancellation of the offer with an apology as well as an admission that "under no circum-stances could she employ a colored girl" (46–47).

Obstacles continued to confront Church Terrell in her adult life. For example, after several years of marriage she and her husband, Robert Terrell, sought to buy a home. She anticipated discrimination in their efforts, knowing that persons of her race confronted difficulties buying homes in any area where "self-respecting people of any color would care to live." Still, even she was surprised at how substantial the obstacles were. Finding a suitable house only one remove from Howard Town, which was almost exclusively a Black community, she was amazed at the refusal of the owner to sell to them. Finally a sympathetic realtor intervened: he arranged a White buyer for the house, who immediately resold it to the Terrells (113–14).

On his part, Robert Terrell, whom she describes as an "optimist from the crown of his head to the soles of his feet," displayed "cool-headed courage [and] a faith that amounted to conviction that somehow or other justice would prevail" in the Senate hearings every four years to reappoint him to a municipal judgeship in the district. Although he was an honor graduate of Harvard and had a spotless public record, southern senators such as Ben Tillman of South Carolina, Hoke Smith of Georgia, and James Vardaman of Mississippi "literally fought him tooth and nail" in their efforts to impugn his honor and prevent his reappointment (260). Southern newspapers joined the fray, depicting him as

> a large, black, repulsive-looking man with very thick lips and a broad, flatnose, sitting on a dais thundering threateningly to a long line of white people standing beneath him, some of whom were women, trembling with fear as they gazed upon this frightful, black terror filling a judge's chair. Under this forbidding picture were the following words which this black horror was represented as hurling at his white victims, while he glared at them like an ogre: "You white folks come up here and git yo sentence." (262)

These incidents do not exhaust the examples provided by Church Terrell about the discrimination and problems members of her race suffered. They are, however, typical of her depictions. In each case her response is balanced and controlled: she is dismayed and often indignant but usually not bitter.[7] Moreover, in almost every case her reports target individuals rather than all Whites. In fact, she often mentions particular Whites who provided help: a friend alerts her father to her plight on the train when she is a child; her Greek professor is supportive despite Matthew Arnold's comments; Sen. Theodore Burton of Ohio speaks in her husband's defense during one reappointment hearing. Another notable feature of these depictions as a group is the dimensions of human life they cover: education, travel, housing, and employment. Taken together, Church Terrell's incidents convey a compelling portrait of the pervasiveness of racial discrimination in the United States.

But she implies that such racism is not a necessary element in the relationships between Blacks and Whites. Before Jim Crow laws, even in the South, relatively peaceful intermingling of the races had occurred. The mention of the locale of her mother's store and her early experiences on the train provide proof of that. And, Church Terrell repeatedly demonstrates, actual contact often dispels or makes blatant prejudice impossible. For example, she uses her friendship with a particular young White woman while at Oberlin High School to elaborate on this issue.

> In the Oberlin High School I formed a friendship which has lasted throughout my life. To the casual observer no two girls could have appeared much more unlike either in personal appearance or in disposition than my friend Janey and myself. To begin with, we differed in race. . . . My friendship with the white girl illustrates a point which I cannot resist the temptation to stress; namely, the advantages of a mixed school. It helped both the white girl and the colored girl to form a close friendship with a girl of a different race. After having been closely associated with a colored girl whose standard of conduct were similar to her own and whose personality appealed to her strongly, that white girl could never entertain the feeling of scorn, contempt, or aversion for all colored people that she might otherwise have had. No matter how strongly representatives of the dominant race might insist that certain vices and defects were common to all colored people alike, she would know from intimate association with at least one white girl that those blanket charges preferred against the whole race were not true. It would be difficult for her to believe that her own particular colored friend was the only exception to the rule laid down by critics of colored people as a whole. . . . On the other hand, no matter how many sins of omission or commission white people might commit against colored people, a colored girl who has enjoyed the friendship of a white girl knows by this token, if by no other, that there are some white people in the United States too broad of mind and generous of heart to put the color of a human being's skin above every other consideration. (33–34)

Church Terrell goes on to bemoan the increasing tendency toward segregation that prohibits such interaction and the failure to teach "mutual forbearance and tolerance" (34). Clearly, her message is that blanket racial prejudice is both unwarranted by facts and unnecessarily destructive. But she also reiterates that such racial prejudice is not a universal fact of life in the United States, and she urges members of her race to control their reactions to it. In the second to last paragraph of her autobiography, she summarizes her own attitude:

> Finally, I want to insist again with all the emphasis that I can command that I have never allowed myself to become bitter. Naturally, I have been pained and grieved that a powerful group of human beings has limited my activities and has prevented me from entering fields in which I should have liked to work. But the blow has been greatly softened by the efforts which broad-minded, justice-loving representatives of that

group have made to give me a fair chance and a square deal. If it had not been my good fortune to come into contact with such people, my life would scarcely have been worth living, and I would have been a miserable woman indeed. (427)

Church Terrell's depiction of the ubiquity of racism and its thoroughgoing impact on the lives of African Americans is rhetorically important. Despite the prevalence of racism, Church Terrell's outlook is optimistic because of her analysis of the problem. In her account individuals in certain circumstances move beyond racial stereotypes. Her life has included numerous harmonious, mutually respectful relationships between the races. To explain why she has sometimes escaped racism, Church Terrell points to the opportunities and advantages she has enjoyed rather than claiming credit for herself. In her narrative she depicts herself as the beneficiary of others' efforts, most notably those of her parents, rather than as the agent who secured advantages through her own will. Moreover, she indicates that these advantages entail a distinctive responsibility for her, albeit within the confines of her feminine roles of daughter, wife, and mother.

A "RARE BIRD"

On June 13, 1904, Church Terrell began her invited address to the International Congress of Women in Berlin with an observation that presaged Barbara Jordan's words to the Democratic National Convention in 1976:

In all this great world gathering of women I believe I am unique in two respects. In the first place, I am the only woman participating in these exercises who represents a race which has been free so short a time as forty years. In the second place, I am the only woman speaking from this platform whose parents were actually held as chattels and who but for the kindly beneficent Providence would have been a slave herself. As you fasten your eyes upon me, therefore, you are truly beholding a rare bird. (204–5)

Church Terrell decided to refer directly to her African American heritage because the participants had been so curious about "die Negerin"; she hypothesized that some had "evidently surmised that she [would have] rings in her nose as well as her ears" (199). (She was the only woman of color to serve as a delegate to the meeting.) Such a misguided anticipation came as no surprise to Church Terrell, for strangers had frequently been startled that her accomplishments and demeanor were possible for an African American.

Church Terrell took little personal credit for her accomplishments. Rather, she indicated both that her achievements suggested the capabilities of her race, which had almost always been thwarted by discriminatory practices, especially slavery, and that they were the result of distinct opportunities she had been offered that far exceeded those of most of her African American cohorts. Her success is a testament to the potential for her race when reasonable opportunities are open to them. On the first page of her autobiography, noting that her baldness as a baby caused her mother some embarrassment among her friends, Church Terrell hints at this view: "But babies who are born under far more favorable condition than those which confronted me when I was ushered into the world do not have all the blessings of life showered upon them. Bald-headed though I was, the fates were kind to me in one particular at least. I was born at a time when I did not have to go through life as a slave. My parents were not so fortunate. I am thankful that I was saved from a similar fate" (1).

With this observation in the background, the impact of slavery and its aftermath becomes an undercurrent in the first sections of Church Terrell's story, particularly as she discusses her own family. For example, she relates how deeply the story of her grandmother's experiences while a slave affected her, causing her to react with "disgust . . . when somebody rhapsodizes upon the goodness and kindness of masters and mistresses toward their slaves in extenuation of the cruel system" (5). But the consequences of slavery in her immediate family extended beyond her beloved grandmother's painful experiences. The horizons for both her parents were severely limited because of their birth as slaves. Her father never went to school "a single day in his life, since there were not schools for slaves" (6). Through his own diligent efforts he taught himself to read by "constantly perusing" newspapers and to write his name. She returns to her father's abilities by describing his acute business sense, which led him to profit from property bought during the yellow fever epidemic in Memphis: "I have gone into detail in this matter to prove how sagacious, logical and far-sighted my father was. Many men who had graduated from college, perhaps, and who had great reputations for keen business acumen lost practically everything they had in a panic, because they did not use their brains as well as did this unlettered, recently emancipated slave who had never gone to school a day in his life" (37–38). Still this "unusually intelligent and thoughtful" man, who "reasoned exceedingly well," suffered the "vices and defects common to men born at that time under similar circumstances, reared as a slave, and environed as he was for so many years" (6). Apparently among those were a violent temper and a fearlessness bordering on temerity. Clearly, Church Terrell sees environment as a crucial factor in shaping personality, no matter how talented a person may be.

Descriptions of her mother provide additional evidence of this view. According to Church Terrell, her mother, an unusually genial woman, had notable artistic talent. She would have, Church Terrell believes, "acquired considerable reputation as an artist if she had had a chance to study in her youth." When she was able to take lessons in late adulthood, "she was thoroughly absorbed in her work and did nothing from morning till night but paint" (8). Constrained in the outlets for her artistic bent, her mother became a hairdresser, with a reputation for excellence and skill among the elite in Memphis. In addition, her business ability allowed her to establish and manage a successful store for hair-care products (9). This shop was in the most exclusive business section of Memphis, a location that Church Terrell felt she would not have been permitted to occupy in the Jim Crow years.

Despite their conflicting personalities, which caused them to separate when their daughter was quite young, and their differences in talent, both parents suffered the repercussions of being denied opportunities in their youth. But both managed to thrive in their business lives. In part because of their experiences and in part because they realized that the South offered only limited educational opportunities for African Americans, Church Terrell's parents decided to send her north to school at the age of six. Since her mother planned to send her on to Oberlin College, she knew a sound educational foundation was essential and chose the Model School, which was connected with Antioch. While she studied there, her mother also insisted that she study two foreign languages; she became proficient enough in German to deliver her 1904 address to the International Congress of Women in that language. Church Terrell thrived in school because she enjoyed studying and was able, with relatively little effort, to stand at the head of her class. Still, because she was the only African American, she felt compelled, even at this early stage of her life, to "hold high the banner of my race" (21).

Despite the pain of separation from her mother, Church Terrell felt her years at Yellow Springs well spent and happy. Of her mother's decision to send her there she wrote: "Fate surely smiled upon me when she influenced by mother to send me to Yellow Springs and place me in a school associated with Antioch College. . . . When I contrast what my educational foundation would have been if I had remained in Memphis and had been sent to the school for colored children, poorly equipped as those schools were then, with what it was in a model school, I lift up my heart in gratitude to my dear mother for her foresight and for the sacrifice she made in my behalf" (27).

Church Terrell's educational good fortune continued during her years at Oberlin, where she enjoyed her active social life fully as much as her studies. She was particularly grateful for the equitable treatment she received at Oberlin. Because of her academic aptitude, further opportunities for study continued to open up for Church Terrell. Always eager to improve her command of languages, she traveled and studied extensively abroad. She delighted in these experiences but remained fully and constantly aware that others were denied the same opportunities, often simply because of their race. Recalling her reaction to seeing an American flag in Berlin and the flood of patriotism she felt, Church Terrell nonetheless considers how unequal opportunity was in her beloved country:

Then, involuntarily, I thought of the rights, privileges, and immunities cold-bloodedly withheld from colored people in the United States which practically everybody else is allowed to enjoy. . . . The injustices and discriminations of many kinds rushed through my mind like a flood. I thought of the many fine women and men who, solely on account of their race, are debarred from certain pursuits and vocations in which they would like to engage, for which they are splendidly fitted by education and native ability, and in which they would achieve brilliant success, if they only had a chance. (98–99)

A series of fortunate circumstances had given Church Terrell chances that few of her race had. And she had used them to the fullest for her personal development. She hoped to begin a career as a teacher, an occupation that was both congenial to her and socially useful. Having avoided many constraints common to her race, Church Terrell still faced the challenge of crafting a socially meaningful life as a woman in a society with rather rigid gender roles. Her success in balancing her commitment to the advancement of her race, her sense of personal ambition, and her roles as daughter, wife, and mother made her a model for other African American women struggling with the same issues.

THE NEW COLORED WOMAN:
BALANCING RESPONSIBILITIES AND ROLES

Throughout her years of education and travel, Church Terrell had set a clear goal for herself: "I had consciously availed myself of opportunities for preparing myself for a life of usefulness as only four other colored women had been able to do. . . . All during my college course I had dreamed of the day when I could promote the welfare of my race" (60). But fulfilling this lofty ambition was not without problems because Church Terrell, as were many women of her day, was acutely conscious of her gender roles. Thus, before she could help others climb, she first had to find ways to negotiate the tensions between her roles as a woman and her personal goals. For Church Terrell this process included at least three phases: first, coping with her father's expectations for her, then resolving the conflicts between her desire for a family of her own and her professional life, and, finally, finding outlets for her energies that were consonant with her responsibilities as a wife and mother.

When she returned from a trip to Europe to live with her father and his second wife in a "beautiful Queen Anne house," she found her comfortable life unfulfilling. To her mind, she was leading "a purposeless existence" (59). The cause of her enforced idleness was her father's attitude, which derived from his notions of ladylike behavior. A self-made millionaire, her father was opposed to women working, except out of financial necessity. From his perspective, his ability and willingness to provide well for his daughter exempted her from a need to work. Although Church Terrell acknowledged that her father's viewpoint accorded with prevalent attitudes in southern society, she refused to acquiesce. Her refusal is doubly significant; not only did she reject the guidance of her father along with his financial protection, a bold stance for a woman of her day, but she also refused to fill a comfortable, secure role that would have been the envy of many middle-class women. She warranted these actions by her dedication to advancing her race.

Despite her father's stringent objections, Church Terrell accepted a position at Wilberforce University, but her choice reflected her effort to compromise with him: she chose a northern rather than a southern school, believing he would see that as less objectionable (60). During her first year at Wilberforce, her father refused to communicate with her. Moved by a sense of filial responsibility, Church Terrell initiated reconciliation, but without compromising her desire to pursue a career.

Because of the daunting workload at Wilberforce, Church Terrell left after two years. After another trip to Europe, she accepted a position teaching languages in the public schools of Washington, D.C. This career aligned perfectly with her talents and her social commitments; she found the work stimulating and rewarding. Moreover, teaching was an appropriate profession for a woman of her social standing.

But her stint as an independent professional woman was brief. Her supervisor and fellow teacher was Robert Terrell, an honor graduate of Harvard who was later to become a federal judge. Their mutual interests blossomed, and they were soon engaged. After their marriage her husband secured a position with the federal government. Her autobiography contains no hint that she considered continuing to teach after her marriage or that she resisted the pressures to become a full-time wife. However, an unsought opportunity did tempt her to change her plans. Shortly before her marriage she received an offer to return to Oberlin as registrar, which stimulated a deep conflict in her. She considered postponing her marriage for a year to take the job. Her narrative of these events reveals the tensions she experienced among her personal ambition, her commitment to her race, and her sense of herself as a woman.

> I wondered whether the letter was genuine when I read it. I had never dreamed of securing such a position in an institution of Oberlin's standing. It had never occurred to me that any colored woman, however great her attainment might be, would be considered in the search for officers or instructors in a college for white youth in the United States. Although I had promised definitely to marry the following October, it was a great temptation to postpone my wedding and go to Oberlin as registrar. . . . The day I wrote declining the position I was very unhappy indeed. . . .

It is quite possible I made a mistake in not becoming registrar of an institution which was attended mainly by white students and in which each member of the faculty was white. It may have been my duty to establish such a precedent in a white college of Oberlin's standing as that undoubtedly would have been. It might have encouraged other institutions to recognize their colored alumnae. If I acted unwisely, I am sorry, although regrets do no good now. In declining to become registrar of Oberlin College, whether I made a mistake or not, I certainly deprived myself of the distinction and honor of being the first and only colored woman in the United States to whom such a position has ever been offered, so far as I am able to ascertain. (103)

Church Terrell's decision to proceed as planned with her marriage indicates her continuing efforts to balance her sense of her roles as a woman with her broader commitments. At twenty-eight, Church Terrell had experienced a rather long period of personal independence. Her decision to marry and begin a family necessitated her surrender, at least temporarily, of her personal ambitions. As tempting as the alternatives were, family life was clearly important to Church Terrell. The Terrells' first three babies died shortly after birth; these losses were extremely depressing but did not end her efforts to have a child. Noting that these deaths were a "great blow" to both her and her husband, she admits: "The maternal instinct was abnormally developed in me. As far back as I can remember I have always been very fond of children" (106–7). The death of her third child was especially difficult for her, in part because the hospital where the baby was born, presumably one for her race, lacked an incubator and the improvised one available was ineffective. Also, she learned of the lynching of a close friend during her third pregnancy, and Church Terrell confesses that the "horror and resentment felt by the mother, coupled with the bitterness which filled her soul, might have seriously affected the unborn child" (108).[8]

Finally, with one daughter of her own and the adoption of another, Church Terrell went about raising her children in a racist society. But her role as mother intensified her sense of the problems confronting her race. For example, she mentions how she missed enjoying certain activities with her children because of her reluctance to "hoodwink" the persons in charge into believing they were White in order to gain admission. She also encouraged her children to resist injustice through any legal and moral means in order to secure for themselves the benefits to which they were entitled, even though others would deny them because of their race (246).

Much like Cady Stanton, Church Terrell relates some of her experiences as a homemaker. But unlike Cady Stanton, she is candid about her initial ineptitudes.[9] Despite her early failures, some comically related, she mastered the culinary arts and admits that she enjoyed cooking as well as other domestic chores. In fact, her mother's admiration and pride in her skills as a jelly maker provide a segue for Church Terrell to rationalize her decision to become more active outside the home. Her mother boasted of her daughter's skills as a homemaker to Frederick Douglass, whom she met on a streetcar. His response "took Mother back considerably":

> Instead of enthusing over the fact that I spent so much time and strength in doing such work, Mr. Douglass, who was one of my best friends, stated in no uncertain terms that he thought I was making a great mistake. He thought it was a pity, he said, that I could not devote more of my time and strength to the work for which I had been trained and which I seemed to enjoy. Public work of various kinds was my forte, he said. There were comparatively few colored women at the time who could discharge those duties . . . and if the few who could were going to use themselves up in drudgery, the race would be the loser and the sufferer in the end. "Try to persuade your daughter to use her head," he said, "and let others whose brains have not been trained use their hands." Mother was very much impressed with Mr. Douglass's advice, for she had often expressed an opinion similar to his herself. (125)

In response to Douglass's comments, Church Terrell defended her behavior by citing her domestic responsibilities which, even when she had help, she could not abandon. However, Church Terrell did find a way to accommodate his suggestion by drawing on help from her mother: "I was able to leave home to fill lecture engagements occasionally, which I could never have done with a clear conscience but for her presence in the home" (126).

Like many middle-class, relatively affluent women of her day, Church Terrell had an active life in the public arena without pursuing a career. Relatively early in her married life she was appointed to the School Board in Washington, D.C., a position for which she was distinctively qualified since she was the only member who had actually taught in the schools. Although her tenure on the board was not without controversy, many citizens attended a testimonial in her behalf at the end of her term. She had been an ardent supporter of woman suffrage from her college days and before her marriage had indicated her support for votes for women at a public meeting. In fact, when her future husband teased her that such public demonstrations for suffrage would destroy her chances of finding a husband, she retorted that she would not care to marry a man who did not support the measure (144). She became an active participant in woman suffrage activities, even addressing the national conventions. In fact, she recalls that the first favorable press review she received for a speech was for a 1900 address, "The Justice of Woman Suffrage." The *Boston Transcript* called the speech "able and brilliant," particularly citing her "earnest argument, biting sarcasm and delightful raillery." A later editorial in the paper pointed to one passage in her speech as "the most striking and concise statement of the whole session" (146–47).

Learning from her attendance at woman suffrage meetings, she helped organize and served as chair of the Educational Committee for the newly organized Colored Woman's League. Shortly thereafter, when this group merged with the Federation of Afro-American Women to become the National Association of Colored Women, Church Terrell served as the first president. This organization, modeled somewhat on its counterpart among White women, was dedicated to collecting "all facts obtainable to show the moral, intellectual, industrial and social growth and attainments of our people [and to] promote the interests of colored people in any direction that suggests itself" (150). The National Association of Colored Women sponsored a host of improvement activities, including night classes for adults (some of which Church Terrell taught) and kindergartens. Church Terrell and the association were particularly concerned with the family. In her first presidential address, she averred that "it is only through the home that a people can become really and truly great."[10] A bit earlier in the address Church Terrell had noted that the association was comprised entirely of women "not because we wish to deny rights and privileges to our brothers in imitation of the example they have set for us for so many years, but because the work which we hope to accomplish can be done better, we believe, by the mothers, wives, daughters, and sisters of our race than by the fathers, husbands, brothers, and sons" (134).

Church Terrell was also a charter member of the NAACP and remained active in that organization until near the end of her life. With the advent of World War I, she entered government service work in response to a national call for help, but a series of racially discriminatory experiences forced her resignation because staying in such an environment was "abhorrent" to her (259). A lifelong Republican, she took the opportunity provided by the passage of the Nineteenth Amendment to organize African American women to vote. Her efforts in this direction led to her appointment at the National Republican Headquarters to direct work among women of her race (309).

This brief summary does not do justice to the range of Church Terrell's activities nor the impressive record she amassed as a private citizen in public service. Still, it does indicate how successfully she combined an active life of public service with her roles as wife and mother. Although her activities were widespread and diverse, certain threads unite them. Consistently Church Terrell sought out opportunities to be socially useful and to work for the benefit of her race. Her activities focused on education, concern for issues related to the family, opposition to blatant discrimination, and efforts to extend suffrage. Usually without remuneration, she worked constantly to improve the conditions in her community and to advance her race. Galled by the opposition she confronted because of the rampant racism, she nonetheless refused to become discouraged and abandon the struggle. Her life became a paradigm of social commitment and constructive, firm action.

Her depictions of how she coped with the dual barriers of her race and gender reflect three interesting and, I would argue, "feminine" rhetorical strategies. First, as she explains her successes, she carefully indicates that she has had opportunities and advantages not typical for others of her race, which have enabled her to overcome many obstacles. Rhetorically, Church Terrell deflects attention from her own attributes in explaining her success, a strategy that suggests a becoming, womanly modesty. Second, Church Terrell grounds her defense of her social activism by arguing implicitly that her opportunities and privileges entailed responsibilities for the improvement of her race. Her sense of duty becomes an impetus for her work as a social activist. Much as earlier women's rights activists had, Church Terrell warrants her social activism through an appeal to moral responsibility. Finally, the venues in which Church Terrell initially pursued her efforts to improve her race were ones suitable for a "respectable" middle-class woman of her day. Only late in her life, years after writing her autobiography, did Church Terrell move from decorous activities to confrontation. In essence, she crafted a narrative that reveals her sensitivity to issues related to gender roles and suggests, through her own example, how other women might negotiate the tensions between feminine decorum and social activism.

"LIFTING AS WE CLIMB":
AUTOBIOGRAPHIES AS DEMONSTRATION AND EVIDENCE

The motto of the National Association of Colored Women, "Lifting as we climb," is a fitting description of Church Terrell's public life. In 1932 Oberlin placed her on a list of its most famous alumnae, an especially welcome honor given her great respect for and gratitude toward her alma mater. On her ninetieth birthday seven hundred people gathered at the Statler Hilton to celebrate her contributions.[11] At that meeting Walter White, then president of the NAACP, praised her longtime devotion to the causes; and in 1949 the Americans for Democratic Action honored her for her work against segregation. Her obituary in the *Washington Post* on July 25, 1954, labeled her "a fighter for freedom and human equality." First lady Mamie Eisenhower opined that she was "an example for emulation by all who love their fellowman."[12] Clearly, Church Terrell, who had become increasingly confrontational toward the end of her life, nonetheless inspired admiration and respect from many persons.

The motto also suggests how Church Terrell perceived her life, as she recorded it in her autobiography. In previous chapters we have examined the resources of autobiography as a rhetoric and how some authors have drawn on those resources, whether successfully or not, to complement their public arguments. In the cases of Shaw and Cady Stanton, we saw how the narrative form of autobiography allowed them to depict the emergence of their ideology from real-life experiences and then to enact the model of a new, enfranchised woman. In their stories they were able to refute allegations about the impact of woman suffrage on women by revealing themselves as womanly women. Certainly Church Terrell's autobiography reflects these same strategies. Her narrative also incorporates incidents that demonstrate vividly the racism prevalent in American society, much as Cady Stanton and Shaw convey their assessments of the problems confronting women by depicting episodes from their own lives. And like Willard, Church Terrell crafts an attractive persona by creating a compelling personal mythology.

But because she was writing as an African American woman, Church Terrell's autobiography does more. The work makes a powerful statement on a continuing controversial issue in American life: the validity, implications, and solutions to racial stereotypes. Caught in a racist society, Church Terrell addresses, by the very act of writing, the issues surrounding racism. In effect, her autobiography is a testimony to the power of an individual to shape her life personally as well as publicly, regardless of substantial obstacles. Church Terrell's implicit argument is that, despite its prevalence and strength, racism is not an insurmountable problem in American society. As individuals, members of her race can circumvent some of its devastating effects. As members of groups, they can work to alleviate the bases for racial demonstration. Church Terrell's self told story suggests strategies for combating the racism in this country and demonstrates the success of those approaches.

Her autobiography is a response and rebuttal to widespread contemporary stereotypes about African Americans in general and African American women in particular. The child of former slaves, Church Terrell clearly demonstrates the potentials of her race when educational and social opportunities are available to them. The record of her life is, thus, a clear rebuttal to rampant notions about the inherent inferiority of African Americans. Her dignity, self-discipline, decorum, and emotional balance, as conveyed in many anecdotes in her autobiography, provide proof positive of how successfully African Americans could meet all the expectations of civil middle-class society. In a sense, Church Terrell's life is an exemplar for what William E. B. DuBois had foreseen in his calls for the education of the talented tenth. Her autobiography is a document, not unlike Frederick Douglass's, that attests to the intellectual abilities of her race and which speaks forcefully against stereotypes of innate racial inferiority. Indeed, the narrative of her extraordinary accomplishments, which are completely appropriate in an autobiography, provides a powerful interpretative frame for the incidents of racism she herself encountered. In the context of her successes and accomplishments, these racist incidents appear particularly unwarranted.

Equally important rhetorically, Church Terrell's self-told story models how a member of a marginalized group can, quite successfully in her case, resist social constraints. Despite repeated confrontations with prejudice and discrimination, Church Terrell retained her personal dignity and her emotional balance. She did not, as she repeatedly avers, become bitter. Of course, she was able to maintain her equanimity in part because she had tremendous educational and financial resources not available to many persons. But in part, she coped successfully because she refused to accept the stereotypes and constraints that others sought to impose.

She firmly insisted on charting her own course, sensitive to but not controlled by what others wished her to do. But, significantly, she did not compromise her principles. For example, in World War I she resigned her position because of the hostile, discriminatory atmosphere in the work place. Confronting a superior to protest an order to ban African American women from a lavatory they had been using, Church Terrell proffered her own resignation. He hesitated to accept it, asking her to reconsider in part because she had indicated explicitly that the reason for her resignation was the humiliating treatment of these women. She agreed to alter her reason if he would rescind the order; he agreed. Having won her point and saved the women from embarrassment, Church Terrell nonetheless stuck by her resignation, although she admits that the loss of the income was significant (257–59). The mode of her resistance in this matter, as in others, was calm and restrained, rather than belligerent and confrontative.

On various occasions, notably during hearings about her husband's reappointment as a federal judge, Church Terrell lobbied influential individuals personally. Again, she realized that a moderate tone, personal dignity, and reason were powerful weapons in the struggle. Her letter seeking the support of Sen. Theodore Burton from Ohio is a model of strategic pleading. The penultimate paragraph, following a careful delineation of her husband's merits, hints at her rhetorical skill and models the kind of strategies she espoused for dealing with racism:

> Busy as you are, it is wrong to inflict such a long letter upon you. As kind as you are, it is inconsiderate, perhaps, to tell you such a tale of woe. I feel, however, that it is my duty to let you see the chamber of horrors and injustices through the eyes of one of the victims. I am sure you will do everything in your power to see that my husband is confirmed. A great principle is at stake. It does not seem possible that the Senate of the United States intends to serve notice on colored people that no matter how able, worthy or successful some of their representatives may be, he shall receive no recognition at their hands, but shall be driven from any position of honor or trust that he may hold. (265)

Significantly, Church Terrell was successful in this case as she was in others. Indeed, the next chapter in her autobiography details her success in persuading the secretary of war to suspend an order against three companies of African American soldiers who refused to indicate which of their number had "shot up" Brownsville, Texas. She records how she became involved in this effort to secure justice and cites press stories to attest to the impact of her efforts (268–72). The last half of her autobiography is replete with examples of the impact of racism in the lives of her fellow African Americans and her efforts to deal with this issue forthrightly. By narrating events as part of her recollections she can both demonstrate her approach and indicate its effectiveness in a not so subtly didactic way.

As distinguished as Church Terrell was, she was not alone in the path she pursued. Indeed, many women of her race turned their energies to social improvement activities. As the sociologist Sharon Harley observes: "The vast majority of local black teachers and former teachers who involved themselves in the women's club movement outside the traditional sphere of female public activities—the church—did so because they believed, as did most formally educated women of the time, that they had a special responsibility to their respective communities, which they alone could fulfill."[13] However, combining this commitment with their responsibilities to their families was challenging. In her study of black women in American society, Paula Giddings points to Church Terrell, Ida Wells Barnett, and Mary Murray Washington as three women who struggled successfully with this challenge.[14] Another function of Church Terrell's autobiography, then, is to offer the record of her life as a model for other women who struggle with the dual obstacles of race and gender. Certainly, the resources of narrative make it a suitable vehicle for such a demonstration. That Church Terrell persisted in her efforts to find a publisher for her work and that in it she specifically notes her sense of facing dual obstacles are strong suggestions that she saw her book as speaking particularly to women of her race.

Certainly, Church Terrell had addressed the issue of racism repeatedly and forcefully in her lectures and writing; the attitudes she conveys in her autobiography do not differ substantively from the views she expressed in her public rhetoric. However, the venue of autobiography opened additional possibilities for her to communicate her message. Crucial to Church Terrell's effectiveness in responding to racism in her autobiography are her rhetorical tone and persona. While her insistence that she has not become bitter may wear a bit thin, she nonetheless exhibits a sense of balance and perspective. At times she reports events with a touch of ironic humor, amused as well as disgruntled with the episodes she relates. At times her recollections bristle with anger, but it is always a righteous indignation with which a reasonably sympathetic reader can empathize. Petulance, whining complaints, and unrestrained malice are completely absent from Church Terrell's story. The persona that emerges in this narrative is a dignified, principled, admirable woman who seeks consistently to advance her race. Church Terrell uses the resources of personal narrative to demonstrate her attitudes in action as she lives her life.

Church Terrell's autobiography seems empowering and optimistic. Her analysis of the nature of racism and her responses to it paint a rosy picture of an individual's ability to cope with the constraints she faced. However, one might reasonably question whether Church Terrell's life story does speak forthrightly about racism in the United States. Her unusual background, including a fine education and financial security, make her story far from typical for her race. On one level hers is an elitist story, in which economic forces help her overcome barriers that would be insurmountable for less fortunate persons. Her experiences are far removed from the physical and psychological suffering endured by most of her contemporary African Americans. Rhetorically, readers might assess her story as lacking narrative fidelity: her successes might not accord with their own experiences.

In crafting her story, however, Church Terrell forestalls that reaction to some extent by relating incidents in which racism thwarted her efforts—something less affluent readers could certainly respond to—and by acknowledging her good fortune explicitly. Moreover, her strong sense of responsibility for the advancement of her race, which runs through the book, indicates her keen awareness of the plight of less fortunate persons. She does not offer her life as a typical story; in contrast, for example, Frederick Douglass's experiences, as unusual as its author was, did purport to be largely typical for slaves of the time.

In sum, Church Terrell provides a glimpse of the possibilities for her race if the force of racism can be constrained. To her peers, her life story provided a clear record of achievement that they could admire and emulate. To others, her story was "a great beacon of hope to millions of Negro[es] . . . who had been seared in the flames of withering injustice." [15]

CHAPTER 7

WHEN AND WHERE I ENTER

Autobiographies as Public Rhetoric

LIVES AS ARGUMENT

In the preceding chapters I have indicated some arguments that women's autobiographies advance, albeit indirectly.[1] But let us step back a bit further and focus not on the particular arguments but rather on *how* these works argue and their function in the public arena. Obviously, these works are complex and varied; they offer a myriad of details about these women, their relationships with others, their activities, and their attitudes. But I would argue that these details construct a remarkably similar argumentative structure in these narratives.

In an overview of his dramatistic method, Kenneth Burke raises a question that is useful in explicating the recurrent argumentative structure I perceive: "What is involved, when we say what people are doing and why they are doing it?"[2] Burke's goal is to explore how language reveals motives and how rhetors use language to build cooperative action. Burke answers this question in part by noting that "any complete statement about motives will offer *some kind of* answers to these five questions: what was done (act), when or where it was done (scene), who did it (agent), how he did it (agency), and why (purpose)."[3]

From this framework autobiographies portray the actions and explain the motivations of the authors. In recording her/his life an author seeks to find coherence and meaning in the events recounted. Unlike the writing of a diary entry, the autobiographical act construes lived experiences into a pattern. For a person deeply involved in a cause—as were the women whose works I have studied, writing a life is an accounting for decisions and actions. To adopt Burkean terminology, these authors depict themselves as agents who act in specific ways (agency) in particular circumstances (scene) to accomplish a clear end (purpose). Thus, for example, in her autobiography Willard displays herself as a woman crusading for the elevation of society through temperance. Church Terrell portrays herself as a "colored woman" seeking useful activities to help others and elevate her race.

In every case these authors depict themselves as agents who struggle against a scene of injustice and inequality. Indeed, their direct, painful experiences with this oppressive scene motivate them to action. However, although they are victims of the injustices and problems against which they are protesting, their struggles and efforts are largely for the benefit of others. Without exception, as they write their lives, their efforts have not been fully successful. Woman suffrage, racial justice, and temperance remain elusive, although still compelling goals.

From a Burkean perspective, these works focus on agent, scene, and purpose. These women write their lives solely because they have been major participants in causes larger than themselves. They do not claim individual distinction; rather it is their devotion to and activities for causes that make their lives worthy of recording. Their actions and, indeed, their entire lives must be seen in the context of a struggle to correct long-standing social ills. The tension between the scene—what is—and the purpose—what ought to be—becomes the explanation for their controversial activities and behaviors. In their depictions they become the agents who struggle to alter the scene.

In Burke's discussion of the pentad, he contends that each element is associated with a particular philosophical school.[4] When a rhetor highlights that element in a depiction, she implicitly seeks the audience's agreement to a particular philosophical orientation. The philosophical schools associated with scene, agent, and purpose are, respectively, materialism, idealism, and mysticism.[5] Obviously, these philosophical positions are complex, and each embraces a wide range of views, some of which Burke elucidates in his discussion. High points of that discussion are helpful for the discussion here.

Of scene in general, Burke notes that the materialistic philosophy emphasizes the importance of material conditions, factors external to the agent, as the best explanation of situations.[6] In other words, an emphasis on scene suggests that conditions in the world constrain human action and decisions. In contrast, agent is associated with the philosophy of idealism, which assumes "the universe throughout to be the work of reason and mind."[7] Purpose suggests mysticism, the mark of which is an assertion of the "unity of the individual with some *cosmic or universal purpose*."[8]

From this perspective, the women studied here create an optimistic view of human existence. In the face of a hostile scene that constrains human activities, they depict themselves as powerful individuals striving to achieve lofty goals. In effect, these depictions emphasize an idealistic view of human existence: individuals can, when guided by a cosmic or moral force, make a difference in the world. They envision and work for a better situation; and their depictions suggest that people are capable of significant actions to improve the conditions for all human beings. This common pattern of depiction suggests how these works argue in a broad sense. These women are agents for a larger group that seeks social justice. In these narratives current social patterns and institutions constitute an oppressive environment in which at least some individuals cannot prosper and develop fully. This oppressive scene becomes an exigency to which these women as moral persons must respond. In short,

104

they become social activists because the scene impels them to act to assure a noble goal.

From a rhetorical perspective, this pattern is strategically wise. By directing attention to the tension between scene and purpose, the authors cast themselves as moral agents. Even if the reader lacks sympathy for the particular cause advocated, the author is seen as an admirable figure who endures struggle and hardship for a goal beyond herself. Such sacrifice and dedication can inspire followers to sustained action, resolving that such efforts shall not have been in vain.

Moreover, and equally important, the tension between scene and purpose grounds the author's decision not in vanity or self-seeking but rather in moral and ethical imperatives. Again, the reader may disagree with the cause but still admire the advocate. That the works studied here had that impact is clear from their reviews; as we have seen, reviewers, even those not in sympathy with the agendas of the authors, generally commented favorably on the character of the women.

This pattern of scene vs. purpose compelling moral agents to act is not common to all autobiographies. Some highlight the extraordinary efforts of the author to elevate herself and realize her potential; others reveal a struggle to determine a course of action, to come to understand what purpose should control a life. The pattern I perceive may, however, be common to many "oratorical" autobiographies in which the author seeks to convey her life as "an idealized pattern of human behavior."[9] Let us examine more closely how these women depict themselves and their purposes as they seek to influence their readers.

WOMEN AS AGENTS:
THE RHETORICAL PERSONA OF THE IMITABLE LEADER

Leadership in the public arena has traditionally been a male prerogative, and the characteristics of male leaders are well-established; among them are courage, dynamism, strength, forcefulness, good sense, and moral rectitude. The qualities that were deemed admirable in middle-class women in the late nineteenth and early twentieth centuries—piety, purity, domesticity, and submissiveness[10]—marked them as unsuited for life in the public sphere, especially for any position of leadership. This group of women made up the target audience for the works studied here. Thus, these authors had to develop rhetorical personae that would both appeal to and empower their readers.

Each of these women crafted a distinctive public image that reflected her individual experiences. But as a group, the rhetorical personae of these women share a number of features, notably: devotion to family and home; persistence and strength of character in confronting obstacles as they pursued their goals; a concern for others that motivated their actions; and an unshakable belief in their own moral rectitude.

FAMILY AND HOME:
THE TOUCHSTONES OF A MODERN WOMAN

First, most of these women depict themselves as committed to family and home, a commitment that reflects their values. With the exception of Emma Goldman, they devote a substantial portion of the initial pages of their autobiographies to discussion of their families and childhood memories. Later, after marriage, most give us glimpses of their own families. Cady Stanton spends a great deal of time discussing the birth and childhood of her first child, although the births of subsequent children receive far less attention. Church Terrell shares her disappointment and pain in the loss of three of her babies. Even Goldman confides that she wanted a child but decided against corrective surgery so that she could devote her full energies to her work.

Willard and Shaw, who did not marry, reveal their connection to children and family in other ways. Willard rhapsodizes over the home and family of her youth; she dedicates the work to her mother—"one royal heart that never failed me yet"—on her eighty-fifth birthday. In "Silhouettes," brief essays reprinted at the end of her autobiography, Willard recalls a conversation with Susan B. Anthony in which they commiserated that "the criss-currents of the world . . . withheld her holiest crown" (motherhood) from them. Anthony, and by extension Willard, took comfort in the fact that their efforts had improved the lot of the women fortunate enough to be mothers. And Willard insists that, nonetheless, women such as Anthony and herself are "mother-hearted." [11] Although her family disapproved of her course of action, Shaw remained loyal to them and includes sections on her parents in her autobiography, most notably a report of her relief at their reconciliation. In fact, the first glimpse she had of the problems confronting women came from witnessing her mother's despair at her father's relocating the family to the wilderness. Her empathy for her mother continued throughout her life. Shaw also relates her efforts to adopt a neglected child, which are frustrated by the alcoholic mother's lack of cooperation. Later in the work Shaw devotes two full chapters to her close relationship with Susan B. Anthony, whom she calls "Aunt Susan." In both tone and substance this section reveals the deep familial connection Shaw felt for her mentor and fellow suffrage worker.

A related theme, home, also emerges in these works. Shaw devotes an entire chapter of her work to her love of home, including several pictures of the house she shared with a woman friend. In her autobiography she alludes to her love of home and how much all suffrage supporters share her attitude. Willard, as noted, frames her entire book with sweet memories of her childhood home, a devotion that persisted throughout her life. Cady Stanton and Church Terrell give us glimpses of themselves as homemakers, in one case supervising child care and in the other describing culinary misadventures, respectively. Church Terrell and Cady Stanton take particular pains to highlight their competence as homemakers and the satisfaction they derived from some domestic tasks. Goldman, who spent almost all her life in transit, speaks fondly of the cottage in Saint Tropez where she spent her final years. Significantly, the discussions of home in these works are not focused on geographical locations; they do not generally rhapsodize about the beauties and benefits of a physical site. Rather, home is a refuge, a place of nurturance and familial contact.

These themes of home and family are not exclusive to women's autobiographies; some men talk of their homes and families, although with a decidedly different focus. On one level the recurrence and treatment of these themes reflect the social constraints that influence all women's lives. Until recently women in our society were strongly encouraged to see themselves primarily as daughters, wives, and mothers. Abundant evidence also suggests that women have traditionally been acculturated to roles of nurturance and support, with the attending focus on relationships. And as Estelle Jelinek has noted, because of societal forces women tend to emphasize the personal in their autobiographies.[12]

But from a rhetorical perspective, their focus on home and family has persuasive force for readers. By articulating their concern for these dimensions of their lives, these women establish their credentials as "feminine" women, women with strong nurturing instincts who to some extent share the interests of their readers. Interestingly, only Church Terrell and Cady Stanton led lives that followed somewhat traditional patterns. Shaw and Willard had long-standing close relationships with other women. The rhetorical personae they crafted in their autobiographies, however, give little indication that any of these women did not fully embrace the values and roles their gender traditionally entailed. In essence, each of these women reveals an awareness of her gender as an element in her identity. These women, no matter how much their public lives and accomplishments set them apart, at least in their autobiographies, suggest that they shared the instincts and interests of their readers. They were, first and foremost, sometimes in different ways, still women. One distinction is crucial here. I do not mean to suggest that the personae these women developed in their autobiographies correspond with their lived experiences and attitudes. Rather, the awareness of gender is a rhetorical feature of the works; whether consciously or not, their depictions of themselves reflect gender as an element in their identity, one that they shared with their women readers.

Not only was gender a key element in the identity of these women, but often it was the warrant for their activities. Cady Stanton, Shaw, Willard, and, in a different but related way, Goldman authorize their participation in agitation for women's rights in their concern for other women, especially in their roles as wives and mothers. Protecting women, the home, and the family as well as empowerment of women became the motivations for these women. In her work on the creation of a feminist consciousness, Gerda Lerner argues that historically women have authorized themselves as agents by appealing to their responsibilities as mothers. She observes, "in the modern period, women would reason their way to claims of equality based on motherhood and later even to group consciousness."[13] Thus, in depicting themselves as women concerned about traditional feminine values, these women were authorizing themselves to speak as women for women. In this way these women negotiate the dilemma that Sidonie Smith sees as facing women who wish to write their lives; she argues that women who assume the autobiographical prerogative transgress traditional notions of femininity.[14] These women carefully crafted their personae as womanly women, concerned about others. It is precisely this womanly concern about others that warrants their autobiographical acts.

Goldman deviates in some ways from the patterns I discussed above. While she does include themes of home and family, her depiction of herself as a woman has distinctive elements. Because she was committed to a new model of womanhood, Goldman reveals her womanliness with different emphases. The new woman she sought to model was keenly in touch with her deepest emotional currents, unlike the sterile professionalism of the "liberated woman" of the day; thus, Goldman frequently pictures herself as nurturer and caretaker. The profession she studied was nursing, a career that combined her nurturing side and her zeal for social usefulness; her work as a nurse led directly to her enthusiasm for birth control because she saw firsthand the suffering of women who must endure unwanted pregnancies or suffer the perils of back-street abortions. On another front, she celebrates her sexuality and her multiple lovers. While she faithfully records her numerous relationships, she does not reveal her jealousy of and obsession with one particular man. Such possessiveness did not accord with the model of the liberated woman that she sought to embody. Thus, even Goldman was conscious of crafting a rhetorical persona that corresponded to "womanhood" as she wished it to be conceptualized. Despite the striking contrast to the more matronly and maternal interests of the other women, these elements in Goldman's work reflect a similar theme: her public role did not preclude her being fully a woman. Indeed, as I argued earlier, her concern for depicting herself as a "liberated" woman in an anarchist sense is a central feature of the earlier pages of her narrative. From a rhetorical perspective, her womanliness, although differently constituted, becomes part of her persuasive strategy.

My highlighting of these women's efforts to depict themselves as womanly women, to fit themselves into prevailing social stereotypes at least to some extent, raises the question of whether only conventional women can be persuasive. It also raises questions about whether seeking out such women to study advances the feminist agenda; one should perhaps locate more women like Goldman, who flaunted social conventions in their desire to be liberated. While I would certainly applaud efforts to explore the lives of other women, those studied here, with the exception of Goldman, chose a particular rhetorical alternative in their autobiographies. Hoping to reach a wider audience, they sought to establish bonds with women who were perhaps uncomfortable with more radical behaviors. Their depictions of themselves in their autobiographies are rhetorical constructs designed, at least in part, to advance a particular political agenda rather than to speak solely to larger issues of women's liberation. Their rhetorical adroitness merits careful study.

Can only conventional women be persuasive? The answer to that question lies in what one means by *persuasive*. Certainly, as Burke suggests, audiences are moved to action by persons they see as like themselves. So, in the short term, conventionality may be a shrewd rhetorical strategy. But as in the case of Goldman, defiant individuals may reach audiences beyond their own day. They may become part of the process of social change and may, in the longer term, have tremendous impact on attitudes and social mores. In short, persuasion in the sense of social change is a complicated process, and, at least in the case of women's issues, altering traditional views of womanhood required a wide range of approaches. The women studied here, including Goldman, all influenced widespread notions of gender and helped redefine what it means to be a woman.

FEMININE COURAGE:
PERSISTENCE IN THE FACE OF OBSTACLES

Another shared feature of these rhetorical personae is persistence and strength of character in pursuit of goals. In the records of their public lives, each of these women details the frustrations and setbacks she endured as she struggled to realize her ideals. For example, Shaw's description of her years in seminary, bereft of the support of fellow students and often hungry, is touching. And she admits she was tempted to abandon her goal of ordination. But her persistence is rewarded when she graduates seminary and goes to her first church.

From the time of her conversion to anarchism, Goldman's life is a sustained struggle against misunderstanding and even persecution by authorities. On one occasion her lover and professional colleague is literally tarred and sagebrushed by local opponents. Goldman herself is twice imprisoned before her deportation. Despite these problems, she refuses to relent.

The lives of Willard, Cady Stanton, and Church Terrell contain less dramatic but nonetheless vivid recollections of the problems they confronted.

Cady Stanton, for example, is deeply upset with the treatment of Lucretia Coffin Mott at the 1840 antislavery meeting in London. Coffin Mott's long-standing and energetic efforts for abolition are well known; the refusal of the male delegates to seat her as a legitimate representative of a female antislavery organization angers Cady Stanton and Coffin Mott but does not diminish their support of the cause.

In reporting their setbacks and frustrations, these women admit their disappointments and discouragements. In affirming their own sense of their lives as worth living, these women do not minimize the difficulties they have confronted. Church Terrell, for example, reiterates the racial prejudices she has endured. Insisting that nonetheless she has had "a fairly fortunate existence," she adds:

> Early in life I realized that a wonderful opportunity was presented to me of rendering valuable service to my own group which needed it. This has helped me face many unpleasant situations and cruel rebuffs with a kind of rebellious resignation and a more or less genuine smile. . . . But never once in my life have I even been tempted to "cross the color line" and deny my racial identity. I could not have maintained my self respect if I had continuously masqueraded as something I am not.[15]

This theme of being true to self despite difficulties emerges in each of these works. These assertions of integrity and personal responsibility highlight these women as moral beings. Even if one disagrees with their causes or particular dimensions of their public lives, one can admire them as upright, courageous women. Their causes have not only secured their enduring commitments, but also have engendered lives of admirable rectitude and public spiritedness. In effect, their records of their commitment to causes they saw as larger than themselves provide strong implicit evidence that the values they embraced are ideal standards for human conduct.

Often, in moments of discouragement, they turn to their female friends and allies for support. Shaw relies heavily on the friendship of Susan B. Anthony and others during her long years on the lecture circuit, as does Cady Stanton. Willard has close female friends who encourage her efforts and sustain her confidence in her work. Church Terrell's husband, mother, and friends such as Frederick Douglass provide both the refuge and the stimulus she needs in her efforts for racial justice. Although she sometimes becomes frustrated with them, Goldman has an array of anarchist friends across the country and internationally who reassure her in the face of adversity.

Despite the obstacles they confront and their natural discouragement at points, none of these women abandons their work. On one level, their persistence stems from their concern for others: each of them sees her work as in behalf of others. Despite harassment from public officials, Goldman continues her advocacy of birth control because she knows from her nursing experience how important the issue is for poor women. Willard sees herself and her fellow WCTU members as protectors of the home; their efforts for temperance will help women who are victimized by drunken husbands.

On another level, each of these women sees her cause as grounded in important principles. For Cady Stanton and Shaw, suffrage is a right of citizenship, guaranteed by the fundamental principles of the republic. Similarly, Church Terrell contends that Jim Crow legislation and practices are in direct contradiction to the Constitution, especially the post–Civil War amendments. Willard, in contrast, sees her work as stemming from Christian ideals. In short, these women portray themselves as moral agents, working in behalf of others to perfect society.

As they recall their busy lives, these women reflect the dynamism often associated with men. Their energy in the home and in the public arena is remarkable. Indeed, in many ways these women are precursors of modern women, who struggle to balance competing demands in their efforts to be successful professionals as well as wives and mothers.

Taken as a whole, these women leaders develop a model of the feminine hero. Some of her virtues—loyalty to home and family, perseverance in the face of obstacles, strength of character, and concern for others—differ from the characteristics typical of most male leaders. And, perhaps more significantly, the feminine hero's virtues represent revisions of and notable deviations from the characteristics associated with the "True Woman" ideal of the nineteenth century: piety, purity, domesticity, and submissiveness. Their reformulation of the virtues of womanhood—except domesticity, which was discussed earlier—merits some examination.

Shaw and Willard, in their professed allegiance to Christianity, demonstrate a piety close to the traditional model. In contrast, Cady Stanton is increasingly hostile toward organized religion; Goldman castigates religion along with capitalism and the political state as enemies of human freedom. Despite their rejection of piety, however, these two women, like the others, evince a principled high-mindedness and concern for others that parallel central tenets of established religion. In essence, their principles, whether religious or personal, govern the behaviors of these women. If some of them are not religiously pious, they are nonetheless ethical persons, whose actions reflect and enact the ideals they endorse.

None of these women challenges traditional notions of purity, with the exception of Goldman; she, of course, celebrates her rejection of entrenched views of sexual morality. In fact, these women omit any mention of their sexuality. Even the married women, Church Terrell and Cady Stanton, give scant attention to their husbands or their married lives. In observing a decorous silence on this issue, these women reflect societal constraints of the time.

These constraints allowed Willard and Shaw to omit discussion of their atypical lifestyles and, thus, to avoid drawing attention to their movement away from traditional roles for women.

Certainly, none of these women reveals the submissiveness often urged as appropriate for their gender. Through descriptions of various incidents, they reveal their assertiveness and sense of self. However, their confrontations are limited almost entirely to their activities in the public realm. Thus, neither Church Terrell nor Cady Stanton dwells on tensions within her home, although strong evidence suggests that Cady Stanton, at least, grew somewhat estranged from her spouse. Shaw, whose family castigated her for her efforts toward ordination, does not dwell on these difficulties. And, indeed, she details her reconciliation with relatives with a sense of relief and joy. In short, these women reserve their assertiveness for conflicts over principle in their public activities.

In effect, in their lives these women enact various new models of femininity that suggest a much wider range for the definition of womanly virtue. As women and leaders, they reinterpret traditional notions of leadership to provide a new image of activism in the public arena.

Imitable Lives: The Committed Woman as Guide

Leaders of controversial social movements must also write their lives as imitable stories. Followers and would-be adherents must see within the examples of the leaders models for their own actions. However, there is a common tendency for an autobiographer to create a personal mythology, to make her/himself the larger-than-life hero of an epic tale. While such an approach may be understandable and perhaps even warranted, an autobiographer wishing to attract followers to her cause should probably avoid that temptation. To cast this in terms of Fisher's framework for narrative rationality, an autobiography that promotes a personal mythology may fail the test of material coherence: the very distinctiveness of the author's life and achievements may make her too lofty for readers to try to emulate. Thus, the test of material coherence that involves a comparison and contrast with other narratives presents a distinctive challenge to the autobiographer. And, again, some negotiate this problem more effectively than others.

Church Terrell, for example, emphasizes the particular advantages she enjoyed as well as the support and encouragement she received from many quarters to explain her remarkable successes. Implicitly, she turns attention away from herself to credit the help of others for her remarkable accomplishments. Willard, in contrast, depicts herself as an agent of God, who was using her as an instrument for his work. While such an explanation for her motivation and accomplishments risks seeming arrogant, Willard cultivates a demeanor of humility and hints at the sacrifices her life entailed, chief among them to be deprived of the crowning glories of marriage and children. The attention to domestic responsibilities and love of the simple life at home are other themes these women employ to build identification with their readers and, at least to some extent, to obscure their exceptionality.

With the possible exceptions of Goldman and Willard, the rhetorical personae developed by these women in their autobiographies provide imitable models for living one's life. Admitting discouragement, acknowledging obstacles, and yet persisting in their efforts, these authors suggest that others can also work effectively to advance the causes. In the cases of Shaw, Cady Stanton, and Church Terrell, readers see women who manage to combine many traditional values with their new allegiances. And one need not become a public lecturer or organizational president to make a contribution; support for an agenda can be on many levels. The only criterion is that one accept the social truths to which she devotes her energies. And because those advancements are framed as modifications, even perfectings, of the existing system rather than radical change, the reader can embrace the cause without undue psychological stress. Finally, because these women depict themselves as much like the readers, their audience is empowered to follow their lead.

Janet Gunn's notion of the autobiographical situation is germane here. As I noted in chapter 2, Gunn sees autobiography as "a cultural act of self reading" with two aspects: the autobiographer reads her life in retrospect as she puts it into narrative; the reader, in turn, considers her life in the light of the messages she perceives in that narrative.[16] In her view, the reader appropriates the text and relates her own life to it. The women studied here facilitate the reader's appropriation of their texts by fashioning largely appealing and admirable rhetorical personae. Thus, even readers who are unable or unwilling to become activists for a cause can nonetheless endorse its goals and support its agenda.

In an earlier work, I argued that the woman suffrage press functioned in part to create a model of the new woman that enfranchisement would both benefit and produce.[17] Over a period of years, in various periodicals, interested women received a clear impression of the progressive woman who sought greater scope for her activities while maintaining an allegiance to some traditional values. I would argue that these autobiographies function in much the same way. They provide images for readers to emulate in an era of changing social stereotypes with regard to gender. Women such as Shaw and Church Terrell developed engaging personae as they narrated their lives. If Cady Stanton and Goldman were a bit more daunting as role models, they nonetheless presented admirable self-portraits to inspire women. While their lives were by most standards extraordinary, these women suggested alternative styles of being women. In doing so, they subtly encouraged their readers to follow their lead.

By articulating the problems confronting them as women or, in the case of Church Terrell, as a member of a particular racial group, these women encouraged others to share their views of the world, to agree with them about the imperfections in the social order that they sought to correct. In essence, while they wrote for an audience, these women through their autobiographies reshaped that audience, bringing their readers to a fuller understanding of important social issues. So, for example, when Church Terrell records an array of experiences of discrimination, totally unwarranted by her character or her behavior, the reader begins to perceive the ubiquity and importance of the issue of race in American society. Goldman's depictions of the abuses suffered by women in sweatshops or by political dissidents alert the readers to a way of looking at the world that they have not experienced before. One significant function of these works, then, is to draw on the resources of autobiography, particularly the power of the author's voice and the chronological structure, to reshape audience perceptions and, thereby, to create an audience for the causes they supported.

TRUTHFULNESS AND THE AUTHOR *IN* THE TEXT

At this point, considering the "truthfulness" of the personae these women develop in their autobiographies is useful. Obviously, any blatant falsehoods would disrupt the autobiographical pact that binds reader with author and that, in my view, intensifies the persuasive force of the genre. However, a rhetorical persona can be a subtle creation. In writing, an author can create a nuanced portrait, one that complements and supplements an existing public image. On the most obvious level, omitting facts or downplaying their importance can create a more favorable slant on personality or action. Goldman's silences about her jealousy are a case in point. But on a less obvious level, the very acts of remembering and interpreting imperil the historical accuracy of the account because the author has a perspective she did not have when the events occurred. As William Howarth explains, the autobiographer "artfully defines, restricts, or shapes that life into a self-portrait—one far different from his original model, resembling life but actually composed and framed as an artful invention."[18] Cady Stanton can, accurately perhaps, portray herself as a diligent housewife in the early years of her marriage. That depiction does not correspond to her role and situation at the time she is writing; in effect, she is creating a truthful fiction that bears only a slight resemblance to the woman she has become. And her understanding of herself in those early years draws on experiences she had subsequently.

De Man questions the very possibility of autobiography, arguing that the nature of the genre controls the author's efforts to depict herself. He observes somewhat cryptically: "Autobiography veils a defacement of the mind of which it is itself the cause."[19] Less cryptically, de Man distinguishes between the author *of* the text and the author *in* the text to suggest that any autobiography creates a fiction: the author who writes her own life reports the past with information and perspectives she did not possess as the events transpired. The reader engages the author *in* the text; the reader assumes at least a correspondence between that depicted person and the narrator of the tale.

Truthfulness in an autobiography poses substantial problems for a historian, who may seek the "facts" of an event. From my perspective the issue is less troublesome. Because Cady Stanton must pick and choose events from her life to record, her report of her early experiences as a housewife is necessarily a rhetorical creation rather than a factual account. As I have explained earlier, readers do test any narrative in relation to the "facts" of an event as they know them. But when an author records her past personal experiences, the reader has no material reality to test those accounts against. Understanding and evaluating those events, readers rely on tests other than "truthfulness" or "facticity." Thus, although I agree with de Man's observations about autobiography as a defacement of the author, the rhetorical persona the author creates can become a reality for the reader, who then must try to judge the value of the narrative.

DEFENDING AN ACTIVIST LIFE: PURPOSE AS MEANING

Activism is not, of itself, an admirable concept. Only when human energies are focused on a cause seen as important do we respect the advocate for it. In establishing the meaningfulness of their lives, then, these women have to demonstrate that the issues they address are salient and merit attention. To provide the reader with an understanding of why they became activists, these women first show that the social situation they confronted was problematic.

In telling their stories, most of these women show how their ideology grew out of early experiences. Recalling anecdotes from their lives and sharing personal experiences enable authors to suggest the relevance and importance of the issues they address. The obstacles thrown in Shaw's way as she sought ordination and the slights Church Terrell experienced in her efforts to find employment or secure a suitable home for her family are convincing examples of the problems that these women addressed in their public lives. These incidents are particularly compelling since they show social constraints and practices as interfering with women who are pursuing admirable activities. Seeking a job in line with one's academic credentials, wanting a pleasant home for one's family, claiming a seat as a delegate to work for abolition, and striving to answer a call to ministry are all admirable human goals. Readers who learn how social stereotypes hindered Church Terrell, Cady Stanton, Shaw, and other women as they pursued these respectable, even admirable activities are subtly encouraged to endorse their efforts for suffrage and racial justice. In short, authors can use narrative to demonstrate how social forces violate shared values and to support a proposal for constructive change.

Recounting a life dedicated to an admirable but still unattained cause raises the question of the value of one's efforts. To work for change, even desirable change, and to have fallen short of achieving the goals one sought may seem a fruitless endeavor, a life misspent. Each of these women affirms, sometimes explicitly, her sense that her life has been worthwhile. For example, Shaw writes in "Vale," the final chapter of her book: "But long or short, the one sure thing is that, taking it all in all, the struggles, the discouragements, the failures, and the little victories, the fight has been, as Susan B. Anthony said in her last hours, 'worth the while.' Nothing bigger can come to a human being than to love a great Cause more than life itself, and to have the privilege throughout life of working for that Cause."[20]

In a similar vein, Willard claims in her final chapter: "I have had the happiness of illustrating in a small way the result of American institutions upon individual and family life, in the hope that good might come of it to some who are now in the formative period of their career; and with the purpose to applaud whatsoever things are true and lovely and of good report, frankly bemoaning those things that are not, in myself especially."[21] While such avowals are both predictable and transparently self-serving, they carry persuasive force in the context of the autobiography. To readers who have read the narratives of these women and who have identified with them as individuals and as representatives of a cause, that they themselves found their lives worthwhile is reassuring.

As mentioned earlier, all of these women state that pressures from friends and interested individuals gave them the incentive to write their autobiographies. On one level, writing one's life in response to the demands of others relieves the author of the onus of asserting the importance of her life on her own. And as Spacks has noted, women have traditionally had difficulty with the act of self-assertion inherent in the autobiographical act.[22] On another level, construing one's decision to write as a response to others' insistence on the importance of one's life underscores both the significance of one's efforts and the value of the cause. Indeed, the very existence of these works serves to confirm the meaningfulness of the lives they record. In effect, the autobiographical act, endorsed and encouraged by others, is the ultimate proof that each woman's work has been of value and importance.

EXPANDING A RHETORICAL SPACE

Arguing both explicitly and implicitly for a greater expanse for women's activities, the women studied here engaged the debate about women's proper roles and responsibilities. The debate was, of course, not a new one. The historian Gerda Lerner traces the roots of what she terms a feminist consciousness to the early Middle Ages, noting that her approximate beginning date of 700 reflects the possibility of documenting women's opposition to patriarchy, not necessarily the first attempts by women to oppose the entrenched masculine perspective.[23] According to Lerner, feminist consciousness "consists (1) of the awareness of women that they belong to a subordinate group and that, as members of such a group, they have suffered wrongs; (2) the recognition that their condition of subordination is not natural, but societally determined; (3) the development of a sense of sisterhood; (4) the autonomous definition by women of their goals and strategies for changing their condition; and (5) the development of an alternate vision for the future."[24] Certainly these women, despite their differences, shared such a consciousness. Their voices as recorded in their autobiographies emerged, however, at a crucial point in the debate about women's roles and responsibilities.

As Lerner notes, the last third of the nineteenth century saw the emergence of organized movements for women's rights, led by the women themselves. The development of such organizations, she contends, indicates that large numbers of women had developed a feminist consciousness.[25] The woman's rights organizations, including such groups as the Women's Christian Temperance Union, provided what Lerner calls sex-segregated social space, "a terrain in which women could confirm their own ideas and test them against the knowledge of other women. Here, they could also, for the first time in history, test their theories in social practice."[26] Karlyn Kohrs Campbell calls the woman's rights conventions of the mid nineteenth century, which substituted for a formal organization before the formation of the suffrage organization, "ideological crucibles," arguing that they served important functions in raising morale and clarifying ideas.[27] In a recent book on feminist epistemology, Lorraine Code uses the phrase "rhetorical spaces" to suggest areas in the midst of the confines of society where sometimes silenced voices can be heard and attended to. "Rhetorical spaces, as I conceive of them here, are fictive but not fanciful or fixed locations, whose (tacit, rarely spoken) territorial imperatives structure and limit the kinds of utterances that can be voiced within them with a reasonable expectation of uptake and 'choral support': an expectation of being heard, understood, taken seriously. They are the sites where the very possibility of an utterance counting as 'true-or-false' or of a discussion yielding insight is made manifest."[28] The meetings, conventions, journals, and

117

newspapers of the women's organizations—of which most of the women studied were members—constituted a rhetorical space where they could discuss and refine their ideologies. Most of the women had enjoyed the advantages of such affiliations and exchanges in the National American Woman Suffrage Association and the Women's Christian Temperance Union—and additionally in Church Terrell's case, the National Association of Colored Women. But although their cohorts within the organizations shared an awareness of the problems confronting women, their ultimate success in achieving their goals depended on spreading their message by moving beyond their organizations to gain adherents. If their various organizations had nurtured and sustained their commitment to woman's rights, securing their goals required attracting new supporters. Their autobiographies reached out for such a new audience and, as I have said, helped create that audience by suggesting a new model of womanhood.

As Campbell has ably demonstrated, women in the first half of the nineteenth century had to struggle for the right to speak from the public platform. By the end of the century they had gained that right, but their role in public life was still marginal. The women who have been the subjects of this work claimed their place in the public arena; their autobiographies reflect lives dedicated to social activism. In telling their life stories, they are not simply recounting their adventures and efforts; rather, they are claiming the public realm as a suitable place for women. Moreover, they are asserting themselves and their view of womanhood into the public arena. In this sense, they were enlarging the rhetorical spaces suitable for a discussion of women's roles and rights by offering their lives as evidence for their claims.

Their autobiographies were not, of course, their only venues for enlarging the rhetorical space for a discussion of woman's rights. Their speeches, their pamphlets, their other writings, and their appearances before legislative committees also moved beyond the sex-segregated groups. But their autobiographies provided a distinctively different vehicle for advancing the cause of women. As I have argued repeatedly in this study, the generic features of autobiography, especially the weight of the author's voice and the bond established between reader and author, provide unusual persuasive opportunities.

A Final Word

As mentioned at the beginning of this book, students of rhetoric have paid relatively little attention to the persuasive nature and force of autobiographies. My discussions will, I hope, stimulate further study and consideration. Any one exploration of a genre as rich and varied as autobiography cannot hope to address most of the issues involved. When one overlaps autobiography with gender issues, the challenges become still more daunting. Still, this is a start. My descriptions, my conclusions, and my thoughts are simply *ballons d'essai,* an invitation to my colleagues for further conversation.

NOTES

CHAPTER 1: AUTOBIOGRAPHIES AS PERSUASION

1. Domna C. Stanton, "Autogynography: Is the Subject Different," in *The Female Autograph,* guest ed. Domna C. Stanton and general ed. Janine Parisier Plottel (New York: New York Literary Forum, 1984), 15. For an interesting rebuttal to this position, see Liz Stanley, "The Knowing Because Experiencing Subject: Narratives, Lives, and Autobiography," in *Knowing the Difference: Feminist Perspectives on Epistemology,* ed. Kathleen Lennon and Margaret Whitford (London: Routledge, 1994), 132–48.

2. Gerda Lerner, *The Creation of Feminist Consciousness: From the Middle Ages to Eighteen-seventy* (New York: Oxford University Press, 1993), 269. Although Lerner's focus extends only to the 1870s, she specifically mentions the autobiographies of Elizabeth Cady Stanton and Frances Willard in the footnote (#65, 327–28) supporting this claim.

3. Barrett J. Mandel, "Full of Life Now," in *Autobiography: Essays Theoretical and Critical,* ed. James Olney (Princeton: Princeton University Press, 1980), 49.

4. Georges Gusdorf, "Conditions and Limits of Autobiography," trans. James Olney, in *Autobiography: Essays,* 48. I am conscious that Gusdorf's use of the term "mythic" reflects what might be termed a masculine view of autobiography. Women's autobiographies may adopt a less self-aggrandizing stance. However, for my purposes, Gusdorf's statement highlights the author's effort to make her life appear as significant ("mythic") and to impose an order on it.

5. Mandel, "Full of Life," 55, 58.

6. Maurice Charland, "Constitutive Rhetoric: The Case of the *Peuple Quebecois,*" *Quarterly Journal of Speech* 73 (1987): 133–50.

7. Charland, "Constitutive Rhetoric," 133.

8. Charland, "Constitutive Rhetoric," 142.

9. Lionel Gossman, "History and Literature: Reproduction or Signification," in *The Writing of History: Literary Form and Historical Understanding,* ed. Robert H. Canary and Henry Kozicki (Madison: University of Wisconsin Press, 1978), 21. Gossman provides a succinct summary of the discussion about the demarcation between the two kinds of writing.

10. Hayden White, "The Historical Text as Literary Artifact," in *The Writing of History,* 42.

11. Louis O. Mink, "Narrative Form as a Cognitive Instrument," in *The Writing of History,* 144–45.

12. Mink, "Narrative Form," 130.

13. Ronald H. Carpenter, *History as Rhetoric: Style, Narrative, and Persuasion* (Columbia: University of South Carolina Press, 1995), 1.

14. Carpenter, *History as Rhetoric,* 1–2.

15. Walter R. Fisher, *Human Communication as Narration: Toward a Philosophy*

of Reason, Value, and Action (Columbia: University of South Carolina Press, 1987), 62–63.

16. Fisher, *Human Communication,* 65–66. The internal quote is from Alasdair MacIntyre, *After Virtue: A Study of Moral Theory* (Notre Dame, Ind.: Notre Dame University Press, 1981), 201.

17. Fisher, *Human Communication,* 47.

18. Fisher, *Human Communication,* 105.

19. Fisher, *Human Communication,* 108–9.

20. There is a lively controversy over the definition of what constitutes an autobiography. The works on which I am focusing are explicitly identified as autobiographies. Thus, while I am in sympathy with a broader definition of the genre, my interest in the rhetorical function of a particular type of autobiography makes the theoretical discussions of the bounds of the genre only tangentially significant to my observations.

21. Kenneth Burke, *Rhetoric of Motives,* 43. Italics in the original.

22. Burke, *Rhetoric,* 55–56.

23. Kenneth Burke, *A Grammar of Motives* (Berkeley: University of California Press, 1969), xv.

Chapter 2: The Nature of Autobiography

1. Albert E. Stone, *Autobiographical Occasions and Original Acts: Versions of American Identity from Henry Adams to Nate Shaw* (Philadelphia: University of Pennsylvania Press, 1982), 3.

2. The *Oxford English Dictionary* cites 1797 as the first usage. In 1809 Robert Southey apparently used the word for the first time in reference to a particular kind of work.

3. Roy Pascal's *Design and Truth in Autobiography* (reprint, New York: Garland, 1985), 21–60; (originally published, Cambridge: Harvard University Press, 1960) provides a succinct, selective history of the genre.

4. James M. Cox argues for an even narrower frame for autobiography: "As I shall suggest, the very idea of autobiography has grown out of the political necessities and discoveries of the American and French revolutions." "Autobiography and America," *Virginia Quarterly Review* 42 (1971): 253.

5. Gusdorf, "Conditions and Limits," 29.

6. The distinction between "true" autobiography and such autobiographical forms as diaries becomes especially salient in considering works written by women who often have experienced difficulty with the self-assertion necessary for such writing.

7. Sidonie Smith, *A Poetics of Women's Autobiography: Marginality and the Fictions of Self-Representation* (Bloomington: Indiana University Press, 1987), 3.

8. James Olney, "Autobiography and the Humanities," proposal submitted to the National Endowment for the Humanities, 1 June 1980, 3. Quoted in Smith, *Poetics,* 3.

9. James Olney, "Autobiography and the Cultural Moment: A Thematic, Historical, and Bibliographical Introduction," in *Autobiography: Essays,* 7.

10. Paul Jay, *Being in the Text: Self-Representation from Wordsworth to Roland Barthes* (Ithaca: Cornell University Press, 1983), 14.

11. Olney, "Autobiography and the Cultural Moment," 4; Jay, *Being in the Text,* 18.

12. Jay, *Being in the Text,* 16.

13. Jay, *Being in the Text,* 21.

14. Jay's formulation runs roughly parallel to Lloyd Bitzer's notion of a rhetorical situation. (Lloyd Bitzer, "The Rhetorical Situation," *Philosophy and Rhetoric* 1 [1968]: 1–14.) As I will discuss below, I believe that certain autobiographies correspond to both a literary and rhetorical exigence.

15. Pascal, *Design and Truth,* 3.

16. Pascal, *Design and Truth,* 3.

17. Pascal, *Design and Truth,* 3, 5–6.

18. Pascal, *Design and Truth,* 9, 11.

19. Pascal, *Design and Truth,* 20.

20. Philippe LeJeune, *On Autobiography,* ed. Paul John Eakin, trans. Katherine Leary (Minneapolis: University of Minnesota Press, 1989), 4.

21. LeJeune, *On Autobiography,* 4.

22. Paul John Eakin, "Foreword," in LeJeune, *On Autobiography,* viii–ix.

23. LeJeune, *On Autobiography,* 13–15.

24. LeJeune, *On Autobiography,* 29.

25. Mandel, "Full of Life," 55.

26. Cf. Jean Starobinski, "The Style of Autobiography," trans. Seymour Chatman, in *Literary Style: A Symposium,* ed. Seymour Chatman (Oxford: Oxford University Press, 1971). Reprinted in *Autobiography: Essays:* "Autobiography is certainly not a genre with rigorous rules. It only requires that certain possible conditions be realized, conditions that are mainly ideological (or cultural): that the personal experience be important, that it offer an opportunity for a sincere relation with someone else" (77).

27. In addition to the works cited below, *Life/Lines: Theorizing Women's Autobiography,* ed. Bella Brodzki and Celeste Schenck (Ithaca: Cornell University Press, 1988) addresses some issues surrounding women's autobiographies and offers case studies to elucidate some of these concerns.

28. Patricia Meyer Spacks, "Selves in Hiding," in *The Tradition of Women's Autobiography: From Antiquity to the Present,* ed. Estelle C. Jelinek (Boston: Twayne, 1986), 112.

29. Spacks, "Selves in Hiding," 113.

30. Estelle C. Jelinek, "Preface," in her *Tradition,* xiii.

31. Smith, *Poetics,* 7–8.

32. Smith, *Poetics,* 8.

33. See, for example: Joe L. Dubbert, *A Man's Place: Masculinity in Transition* (Englewood Cliffs, N.J.: Prentice-Hall, 1979); Elizabeth H. Pleck and Joseph H. Pleck, eds., *The American Man* (Englewood Cliffs, N.J.: Prentice-Hall, 1980); Carroll Smith-Rosenberg, *Disorderly Conduct: Visions of Gender in Victorian America* (New York: Oxford University Press, 1986); Peter G. Filene, *Him/Her/Self: Sex Roles in Modern America* (Baltimore: Johns Hopkins University Press, 1986); Rosalind Rosenberg, *Divided Lives: American Women in the Twentieth Century* (New York: Hill and Wang, 1992).

34. Some men who wrote their life stories during this period may also have struggled with depicting their manhood. However, writing an autobiography had long been

a male prerogative. In contrast, because the act of writing an autobiography intended for public consumption breached traditional notions of womanhood, women faced particular challenges.

35. Smith, *Poetics,* 5.

36. Olney, "Autobiography and the Cultural Moment," 20.

37. Smith, *Poetics,* 5.

38. Smith, *Poetics,* 5.

39. Smith, *Poetics,* 5.

40. See my discussion of Paul de Man's "Autobiography as De-Facement" below. This view seems to parallel his argument.

41. Fisher, *Human Communication.*

42. Arthur Melville Clark, *Autobiography: Its Genesis and Phases* (Edinburgh: Oliver and Boyd, 1935), 15.

43. Clark, *Autobiography,* 22.

44. Clark, *Autobiography,* 21–23. Although the previous chapter has explored the relationships between communication and rhetorical theories and autobiographies, it seems worth noting here that Clark is close to Kenneth Burke's notion of rhetoric as identification and Hugh Dalziel Duncan's ideas of rhetoric as a form of social courtship.

45. William C. Spengemann and L. R. Linquist offer a similar system of categories in "Autobiography and the American Myth," *American Quarterly* 17 (1965): 501–19. In particular, they argue that, influenced by American mythology, autobiographers depict themselves as one of four main character types: prophet, hero, villain, or outcast.

46. William L. Howarth, "Some Principles of Autobiography." In *Autobiography: Essays,* 85.

47. Howarth, "Some Principles," 85. Howarth's view that the life narrated in an autobiography is "far different" from the original model to some extent anticipates de Man's view that autobiographies deface rather than unmask the author.

48. Howarth, "Some Principles," 86. Howarth derives his categories from Northrop Frye's three elements that guide a writer's progress: *mythos, ethos,* and *dianoia.* See Northrop Frye, *Anatomy of Criticism* (Princeton: Princeton University Press, 1957), 52–73.

49. Howarth, "Some Principles," 88–89.

50. Howarth, "Some Principles," 95.

51. Although Howarth does not refer to speech act theory, his categories reflect different speech acts.

52. Howarth, "Some Principles," 105.

53. Pascal, *Design and Truth,* 83.

54. James Olney, *Metaphors of Self: The Meaning of Autobiography* (Princeton: Princeton University Press, 1972), 39.

55. Karl Joachim Weintraub, *The Value of the Individual: Self and Circumstance in Autobiography* (Chicago: University of Chicago Press, 1978), xi, 13.

56. William C. Spengemann, *The Forms of Autobiography: Episodes in the History of a Literary Genre* (New Haven: Yale University Press, 1980), xiii.

57. Spengemann, *Forms of Autobiography,* xiv.

58. Spengemann, *Forms of Autobiography,* 32.

59. Spengemann, *Forms of Autobiography,* xiv–xv.

60. Spengemann, *Forms of Autobiography,* xiii.

61. Patricia Meyer Spacks, "Stages of Self: Notes on Autobiography and the Life Cycle," in *The American Autobiography: A Collection of Critical Essays,* ed. Albert E. Stone (Englewood Cliffs, N.J.: Prentice-Hall, 1981), 44.

62. Spacks, "Stages," 45.

63. Spacks, "Stages," 45.

64. Spacks, "Stages," 45.

65. Spacks, "Stages," 48, 51.

66. Spacks, "Stages," 54.

67. Spacks, "Stages," 59.

68. Spacks, "Stages," 60.

69. Heidi I. Stull, *The Evolution of the Autobiography from 1770–1850: A Comparative Study and Analysis* (New York: Peter Lang, 1985), 12.

70. Stull, *The Evolution,* 12.

71. Janet Varner Gunn, *Autobiography: Towards a Poetics of Experience* (Philadelphia: University of Pennsylvania Press, 1982), 7.

72. Gunn, *Autobiography,* 8.

73. Gunn, *Autobiography,* 8.

74. Gunn, *Autobiography,* 12–13.

75. Bitzer, "The Rhetorical Situation," 1–14.

76. Paul de Man, "Autobiography as De-Facement," *Modern Language Notes* 94 (December 1979): 920–21.

77. Louis A. Renza, "The Veto of the Imagination: A Theory of Autobiography," *New Literary History* 9 (1977): 1–26; reprinted in *Autobiography. Essays,* 269, 274. Cf. Michael Sprinker, "Fictions of the Self: The End of Autobiography," in the same volume: "autobiography, the inquiry of the self into its own origin and history, is always circumscribed by the limiting conditions of writing, the production of a text" (342).

78. Olney, "Autobiography and the Cultural Moment," 22.

79. de Man, "Autobiography," 926.

80. de Man, "Autobiography," 930.

81. Smith, *Poetics,* 6. The material directly quoted is Barbara Johnson, *The Critical Difference: Essays in the Contemporary Rhetoric of Reading* (Baltimore: Johns Hopkins University Press, 1980), 5.

CHAPTER 3: EMMA GOLDMAN AS A LIBERATED WOMAN

1. Candace Falk, *Love, Anarchy, and Emma Goldman* (New York: Holt, Rinehart & Winston, 1984), 122.

2. Falk, *Love,* 122.

3. Goldman to Alexander Berkman, quoted in Falk, *Love,* 3.

4. Falk, *Love,* 122.

5. Richard Drinnon, *Rebel in Paradise: A Biography of Emma Goldman* (Chicago: University of Chicago Press, 1961), 269. I am fully aware that Goldman emphasized anarchism as an antidote for spiritual sterility and emotional repression, especially in

regard to women. But this "spiritual" effect of anarchism was a consequence of its rational analysis and approach to human life.

6. Goldman to Percival Gerson, 2 July 1932, University of California at Los Angeles Collection.

7. Emma Goldman, *Living My Life* (reprint, Salt Lake City, Utah: Gibbs M. Smith, 1982), 3. Subsequent references to this source will be cited as page numbers until otherwise indicated.

8. Paul Avrich, *The Haymarket Tragedy* (Princeton: Princeton University Press, 1984), 215.

9. Avrich, *Haymarket Tragedy,* 215.

10. Ordway Tead, "Emma Goldman Speaks" [review of *Living My Life*]. *Yale Review* (June 1932): 852.

11. Waldo Frank, "Elegy for Anarchism" [review of *Living My Life*]. *New Republic* (30 December 1931): 193.

12. R. L. Duffus, "An Anarchist Explains Herself" [review of *Living My Life*]. *New York Times,* 25 October 1931, IV: 1.

13. Drinnon, *Rebel,* 270–71.

14. Drinnon, *Rebel,* 271.

15. Drinnon, *Rebel,* 272.

16. Letter to Percival Gerson, University of California at Los Angeles Collection, 1932; Drinnon, *Rebel,* 270.

17. Letter to Percival Gerson, University of California at Los Angeles Collection, 1932.

18. Alix Kates Shulman, "Emma Goldman's Feminism: A Reappraisal," in *Red Emma Speaks: An Emma Goldman Reader,* 2nd ed., ed. Shulman (New York: Schocken, 1983), 4.

19. Alice Wexler, *Emma Goldman: An Intimate Life* (New York: Pantheon, 1984), xvii.

20. Drinnon, *Rebel,* 281.

21. Drinnon, *Rebel,* 282.

22. R. A. Preston, unpublished manuscript. (New York Public Library: Emma Goldman papers. No date.)

23. Shulman, "Emma Goldman's Feminism," 4.

24. K. A. Rosenberg, "Emma's Ambiguous Legacy." *Women's Review of Books* (1984): 8.

25. Emma Goldman, "The Tragedy of Woman's Emancipation," in *Anarchism and Other Essays,* 224, 214.

26. Goldman, "Tragedy," 223.

27. Emma Goldman, "Anarchism: What It Really Stands For," in *Anarchism and Other Essays,* 67, 51.

28. Goldman, "Anarchism," 67.

29. Emma Goldman, "Minorities versus Majorities," in *Anarchism and Other Essays,* 78.

30. Shulman, *Red Emma,* 111.

31. Goldman, "Anarchism," 63.

32. Falk, *Love,* 7.

33. Margaret S. Marsh, *Anarchist Women, 1870–1920* (Philadelphia: Temple University Press, 1981), 112.

34. Stone, *Autobiographical Occasions*, 4, 5.

35. Olney, *Metaphors of Self*, 3–50.

36. Olney, *Metaphors of Self*, 261.

37. Thomas P. Doherty, "American Autobiography and Ideology," in *The American Autobiography: A Collection of Critical Essays*, ed. Albert E. Stone (Englewood Cliffs, N.J.: Prentice-Hall, 1981), 108.

38. Doherty, "American Autobiography," 108.

39. Fisher, *Human Communication*, 47.

40. Fisher, *Human Communication*, 105.

41. Fisher, *Human Communication*, 109.

42. Stone, *Autobiographical Occasions*, 23.

CHAPTER 4: FRANCES WILLARD AS PROTECTOR OF THE HOME

1. Joseph R. Gusfield, "Status Conflicts and the Changing Ideologies of the American Temperance Movement," in *Society, Culture, and Drinking Patterns*, ed. David J. Pittman and Charles R. Snyder (Carbondale: Southern Illinois University Press, 1962), 101–20.

2. Ruth Bordin, *Frances Willard: A Biography* (Chapel Hill: University of North Carolina Press, 1986), 112; Ruth Bordin, *Woman and Temperance: The Quest for Power and Liberty, 1873–1900* (Philadelphia: Temple University Press, 1981), 3–4; Bonnie J. Dow, "Frances E. Willard (1839–1898), Reinventor of 'True Womanhood,'" in *Women Public Speakers in the United States, 1800–1925: A Bio-Critical Sourcebook*, ed. Karlyn Kohrs Campbell (Westport, Conn.: Greenwood Press, 1993), 479.

3. Amy Rose Slagell, "A Good Woman Speaking Well: The Oratory of Frances E. Willard." Ph.D. diss., University of Wisconsin—Madison, 1992, 7.

4. Bordin, *Frances Willard*, 129; Joseph R. Gusfield, *Symbolic Crusade: Status Politics and the American Temperance Movement*, 2nd ed. (Urbana: University of Illinois Press, 1986), 93.

5. Gusfield, *Symbolic Crusade*, 93. Two good contextual studies that involve Willard are Betty Boyd Caroli, "Women Speak Out for Reform," in *The Rhetoric of Protest and Reform: 1879–1898*, ed. Paul H. Boase (Athens: Ohio University Press, 1980), 212–31, and Carolyn De Swarte Gifford, "Home Protection: The WCTU's Conversion to Woman Suffrage," in *Gender, Ideology, and Action: Historical Perspectives on Women's Public Lives*, ed. Janet Sharistan (New York: Greenwood Press, 1986), 95–120. Caroli's study parallels the reform work of several late-nineteenth-century women as well as their common problems and approaches. Gifford's study examines the social and rhetorical challenges faced by reformers in the late nineteenth century and by the WCTU specifically.

6. Gusfield, *Symbolic Crusade*, 111.

7. Gusfield, *Symbolic Crusade*, 85; Bordin, *Woman*, 129.

8. Foster led the 1889 walkout of local WCTU groups and became a founding member and first president of the Non-Partisan WCTU. See Blocker, 85. See also Ida

Tetreault Miller, "Frances Elizabeth Willard: Religious Leader and Social Reformer," diss., Boston University, 1978, 79–81; and Mary Earhart, *Frances Willard: From Prayers to Politics* (Chicago: University of Chicago Press, 1944), 222–24. Wittenmeyer was the first president of the WCTU; she privately and publicly disagreed with Willard's ambitious agenda for the organization. When Willard dared to support women's suffrage in a speech at the 1876 national convention, Wittenmeyer apparently told her, "You might have been a leader, but now you'll only be a scout." See Bordin, *Frances Willard,* 103. Earhart calls Clement Leavitt "a veritable Judas" who ran a "campaign of betrayal" (352).

9. Bordin, *Frances Willard,* 223.

10. 26 October 1895, clipped in scrapbook 70, p. 93 (WCTU series, reel 42, frame 142). Bordin (*Frances Willard,* 219–20) quotes the source as the Evanston paper, but the clipping indicates that the original source was the *Chicago Tribune*.Many of the papers of the WCTU are preserved on microfilm. Several of the available rolls are reproductions of original scrapbooks of clippings and news accounts, many of them compiled by Willard's mother and Willard herself. Unless otherwise indicated, I used the original scrapbooks (available in the Willard Memorial Library, housed at the WCTU National Headquarters in Evanston, IL) for this research. Where possible, I indicate where a source from the scrapbook can be found in the microfilm edition (designated as "WCTU series"). See Randall C. Jimerson, Francis X. Blouin, and Charles A. Isetts, eds., *Guide to the Microfilm Edition of Temperance and Prohibition Papers* (Ann Arbor: University of Michigan, 1977). A supplement was published in 1982.

11. Quoted in Lady Henry Somerset, "White and Black in America: An Interview with Miss Willard," *Westminster Gazette,* undated clipping [May 1894], scrapbook 69, p. 20. See also p. 21.

12. Quoted in Alma Lutz, *Created Equal: A Biography of Elizabeth Cady Stanton* (New York: John Day Company, 1940), 275.

13. Bordin, *Frances Willard,* 111.

14. Bordin, *Frances Willard,* 136–37.

15. Bordin, *Frances Willard,* 137. After her autobiography was published, Willard continued to act in "radical" ways. By the mid-1890s, for instance, she "had embraced Fabian Socialism." See Bordin, *Frances Willard,* 129.

16. Welter, "The Cult of True Womanhood," *American Quarterly* 18 (1966): 151–74. See also DeSwarte Gifford and Slagell, who argues, "Nor did Willard's oft-noted 'womanliness' mean that she accepted the ideal of true womanhood—or any other formulations that limited women's role in the world. As she moved from one reform issue to another, she carried with her a constant determination to make the world a wider place for women, and she repeatedly voiced positions that sound strikingly modern in their analysis of women's issues" ("A Good Woman," 50).

17. Karlyn Kohrs Campbell, *Man Cannot Speak For Her: A Critical Study of Early Feminist Rhetoric* (New York: Praeger, 1989), 122. See also Bonnie J. Dow, "The 'Womanhood' Rationale in the Woman Suffrage Rhetoric of Frances E. Willard," *Southern Communication Journal* 56 (Summer 1991): 299.

18. See contemporary testimony to that effect in Slagell, "A Good Woman," 75–85.

19. Frances Willard, *Glimpses of Fifty Years: The Autobiography of an American Woman* (Boston: George M. Smith & Co., 1889). The publication figures are from

Bordin, *Frances Willard,* 116. All subsequent references to *Glimpses* will be cited as page numbers until otherwise indicated.

20. Frances Willard, *My Happy Half-Century: The Autobiography of An American Woman,* ed. Frances E. Cook (London: Ward, Lock & Co. [1894]). By references to *Glimpses* I mean to include both editions of the autobiography, unless otherwise indicated.

21. See Earhart, *Frances Willard,* 226.

22. See *Minutes of the National Woman's Christian Temperance Union* (1888), 66.

23. Slagell, "A Good Woman," 56.

24. The 1894 English version also appeared at a controversial time for Willard, for its publication coincided with Ida Wells Barnett's tour of England, in which she and Willard became embroiled in the lynching controversy. See main text, above.

25. Bordin, *Frances Willard,* 130.

26. See Suzanne M. Marilley, "Frances Willard and the Feminism of Fear," *Feminist Studies* 19 (Spring 1993): 129.

27. See Slagell, "A Good Woman," 56; Helen Tyler, *Where Prayer and Purpose Meet* (Evanston, Ill.: Signal Press, 1949), 101, 105.

28. Source unknown, clipping "Miss Willard's Outburst," scrapbook 70, p. 92.

29. Fisher, *Human Communication,* 47.

30. Campbell, *Man Cannot,* 124, 125; Dow, "'Womanhood' Rationale."

31. See also 605, 607, and 695–97.

32. See Campbell, *Man Cannot,* 9–12.

33. *Denison* (TX) *Democrat,* 12 February 1882 (quoted from scrapbook 15, p. 17 [WCTU series, roll 32, frame 467]).

34. Campbell, *Man Cannot,* 12. Dow discusses Willard's feminine style in her oratory in "Frances E. Willard," 481–82.

35. Jelinek, *Tradition.* The preface to this volume lays out these differences.

36. Jelinek, *Tradition,* xiii.

37. Jelinek, *Tradition,* 99.

38. Willard, *My Happy,* i.

39. Willard, *My Happy,* viii.

40. Bordin, *Frances Willard,* 105.

41. See *Minutes of the National Woman's Christian Temperance Union* (1888), 66.

42. See Miller, "Frances Elizabeth Willard," 89–90.

43. Review of *My Happy Half Century* from [Illegible source for clipping], 29 December 1894, scrapbook 35, p. 14, Frances Willard Memorial Library. Scrapbook 35 is not available on microfiche. It is full of book reviews of Willard's various works, and pp. 14–23 (my numbering) include reviews of the English edition of Willard's autobiography. The compiler of the scrapbook (possibly Willard's mother or Anna Gordon, her companion and secretary) recorded most of the clipping sources and dates in the scrapbook, although many of them are illegible.

44. Review of *My Happy Half Century* from *The Queen,* 9 February 1895, scrapbook 35, p. 21.

45. Review of *My Happy Half Century* [source not noted], n.d., scrapbook 35, p. 23.

46. Review of *My Happy Half Century* from *London Weekly Sun,* 13 January 1895, scrapbook 35, p. 19.

47. Review of *My Happy Half Century* from [city illegible] *Guardian,* 9 January 1895, scrapbook 35, p. 17.

48. Review of *My Happy Half Century* from *Glasgow Herald,* 11 January 1895, scrapbook 35, p. 18.

49. Biographies of Willard include Bordin, *Frances Willard;* Earhart, *Frances Elizabeth Willard;* Anna Adams Gordon, *The Life of Frances E. Willard* (Evanston, Ill.: WCTU, 1921); Gordon, *The Beautiful Life of Frances E. Willard (A Memorial Volume* (Chicago: WCTU, 1898); Lydia Jones Trowbridge, *Frances Willard of Evanston* (Chicago: Willett, Clark & Company, 1938); Florence Witt, *Frances E. Willard: The Story of a Noble Woman* (London: Sunday School Union, [1898]); Bernie Babcock, *An Uncrowned Queen: The Story of the Life of Frances E. Willard Told for Young People* (Chicago: Fleming H. Revell Company, 1902); Ray Strachey, *Frances Willard: Her Life and Work* (London: T. Fisher Unwin, 1912); and Jane A. Stewart, *The Frances Willard Book* (Philadelphia: The Current Syndicate Co., 1906). The Willard Memorial Library has a display of several Willard biographies in languages other than English, including French, Finnish, and Dutch. Briefer biographical treatments include Robert T. Oliver, "Denouncing Demon Drink: Frances E. Willard and John B. Gough," in *History of Public Speaking in America* (Boston: Allyn and Bacon, 1965), 450–59; Elmer C. Adams and Warren Dunham Foster, *Heroines of Modern Progress* (New York: Macmillan, 1929), 215–44; W. T. Stead, "The Uncrowned Queen of American Democracy," *Review of Reviews* 6 (November 1892): 427–44; Lilian Whiting, *Women Who Have Ennobled Life* (Philadelphia: Union Press, 1915), 187–207; and Henry Thomas and Dana Lee Thomas, *Living Biographies of Famous Women* (Garden City, N.Y.: Garden City Publishing Co., 1942), 179–91. Treatments of Willard's rhetoric are available in Slagell, "A Good Woman"; Dow, "Frances E. Willard"; and Richard W. Leeman, *'Do Everything Reform': The Oratory of Frances E. Willard* (New York: Greenwood Press, 1992). Other, more anecdotal and episodic treatments of Willard's personality include Harriet A. Townsend, *Reminiscences of Famous Women* (New York: Evans-Penfold Company, 1916), 32–35; and Anna A. Gordon, ed., *What Frances E. Willard Said* (Evanston, Ill.: WCTU, 1905). Two stories of her childhood are Miriam E. Mason, *Frances Willard: Girl Crusader* (New York: Bobbs-Merrill, 1961); and Clara Ingram Judson, *Pioneer Girl: The Early Life of Frances Willard* (New York: Rand McNally & Company, 1939).

50. See, for example, Gordon, *Beautiful,* 296. See Bordin's discussion in *Frances Willard,* 5.

51. Babcock, *Uncrowned Queen,* 165.

52. Witt, *Frances E. Willard,* 137–38. Witt seems especially interested in minimizing the conflict in Willard's life. On Willard's split with Dwight Moody and his Gospel Crusade in Boston, Witt writes: "Unfortunately, a 'little rift' occurred between Miss Willard and Mr. Moody, which, while it left them friends and warm admirers, dispelled the harmony which had characterized their united work" (72). On the subject of lynching, over which Ida Barnett Wells had publicly and shrilly denounced Willard, Witt writes: "Another evil against which the power of the women was used was the barbarous custom of lynching, and at several of the conventions votes were passed in con-

demnation. Everywhere the coloured population of the States recognized in Miss Willard a warm friend and supporter" (95).

53. See Earhart, *Frances Elizabeth Willard,* 11, and Bordin, *Frances Willard,* 86, 88, 113, 216–18, 221–22. I do not mean to suggest that these biographies are completely negative; they are often very positive in telling Willard's life. They do, however, candidly point out some of her weaknesses, a feature which sets them apart from the early biographies.

54. Scholarly references are few and far between in Willard's early biographies. Still, as Leeman (*Do Everything*) suggests (199), it is not difficult to see that such works tend to show overreliance on her autobiography for pre-1889 material and end up glossing the final years of her life. Later treatments of Willard's life sometimes demonstrate the weakness of the earlier biographies, but secondhand. Some writers, that is, rely on Gordon's biography as their primary source. Since Gordon relies almost exclusively on the autobiography for her narrative, these later works pass on Willard's rhetorical shaping to further generations of readers and researchers. See, for example, Oliver.

55. Olney, *Metaphors of Self,* 43.

CHAPTER 5: ELIZABETH CADY STANTON AND ANNA HOWARD SHAW AS WOMANLY LEADERS

1. Elizabeth Cady Stanton, *Eighty Years and More: Reminiscences 1815–1897* (reprint, New York: Schocken Books, 1971), preface. The title of Cady Stanton's work recalls the title Frances Willard had given her autobiography, published several years earlier: *Glimpses of Fifty Years.* Whether the similarity in titles is accidental or intentional is unclear, but the possibility that Cady Stanton deliberately echoed Willard is intriguing.

2. One biographer, Elisabeth Griffith, specifically notes how Cady Stanton crafted her autobiographical persona: "Like her maternal public image, Cady Stanton self-consciously constructed an appealing autobiography, portraying herself as benign, amusing, undaunted, heroic, and praiseworthy. She admitted to no character flaws and few enemies. She omitted almost any mention of her mother, ignored her husband, misdated events, confused incidents, and forgot scandals" (*In Her Own Right: The Life of Elizabeth Cady Stanton* [New York: Oxford University Press, 1984], xvii).

3. Wil A Linkugel and Martha Solomon, *Anna Howard Shaw: Suffrage Orator and Social Reformer* (Westport, Conn.: Greenwood Press, 1991), 81, 93.

4. Olney, "Some Principles of Autobiography," 95.

5. Other works could be included in this discussion, for example, Abigail Scott Duniway, *Path Breaking: An Autobiographical History of the Equal Suffrage Movement in the Pacific Coast States* (Portland, Ore.: James, Kerns and Abbott, 1914); Charlotte Perkins Gilman, *The Living of Charlotte Perkins Gilman: An Autobiography* (New York: Appleton-Century, 1935). But the status of Shaw and Cady Stanton as elected leaders of the suffrage association and the clear goal expressed by each for

writing their autobiographies make them particularly suitable. The two other presidents of the National American Woman Suffrage Association, Susan B. Anthony and Carrie Chapman Catt, did not write autobiographies.

6. Elizabeth Cady Stanton, *Eighty Years and More, (1815–1897): Reminiscences of Elizabeth Cady Stanton* (London: T. Fisher Unwin, 1898), 33, 71–72. Subsequent references to this source will be cited as page numbers until otherwise indicated.

7. Eleanor Flexner, *Century of Struggle: The Woman's Rights Movement in the United States* (Cambridge: Belknap Press of the Harvard University Press, 1975), 220.

8. Flexner, *Century of Struggle,* 237–39. While one cannot dispute the problems in and limitations of Shaw's tenure as president, Flexner's and others' assessments of her seem unduly harsh. The lack of a national headquarters, organizational problems within the association, and the necessity for Shaw to support herself through lecturing probably account for as many of the difficulties as her personality and limited administrative acumen.

9. Jelinek, *Tradition,* 109.

10. Elizabeth Jordan, "Anna Howard Shaw: An Intimate Study," *Chicago Tribune,* 27 July 1919. This clipping is in the Shaw papers in the Schlesinger Library women's archives at Radcliffe.

11. Anna Howard Shaw, with Elizabeth Jordan, *The Story of a Pioneer* (New York: Harper and Bros., 1915), 19. Subsequent references to this source will be cited as page numbers until otherwise indicated.

12. Jelinek (*Tradition,* 109) draws attention to this fact to support her argument about Cady Stanton's purpose in writing the work.

13. According to Cady Stanton's story, Angelina followed a modern theory about allowing the infant only tiny amounts of food to prevent colic and other problems. When the infant did not thrive, Angelina's sister, Sarah, stepped in and exerted common sense to feed the starving child more adequately.

14. Shaw's failure to mention romances is problematic to interpret. Her collaborator on the work, Elizabeth Jordan, admits freely editing the work to remove anything which would cause Shaw embarrassment or pain. Perhaps unsuccessful romances qualified under these criteria.

15. Cady Stanton reported near the end of her life: "I became a very extraordinary woman, the first of the 'new' women." "Noted Suffragist Reviews Her Life" (clipping, n.d.), cited in Griffth, xx.

16. Flexner, *Century of Struggle,* 216, 217.

17. *New York Times-Saturday Review of Books and Art,* 12 February 1898, 100.

18. Jelinek, *Tradition,* 124.

19. Jelinek, *Tradition,* 71–72.

20. Mandel, "Full of Life Now," 55, 58.

21. Olney, *Metaphors of Self,* 37.

22. Stone, *Autobiographical Occasions,* 3, 5.

23. See Mandel, "Full of Life," 55, 58; Olney, *Metaphors of Self,* 37; Jelinek, *Tradition,* 124.

24. Fisher, *Human Communication,* 104–5.

CHAPTER 6: MARY CHURCH TERRELL AS
A COLORED WOMAN IN A WHITE WORLD

1. The Mary Church Terrell papers at the Library of Congress contain correspondence with publishers and with friends relevant to her efforts to get the book into print. In a letter of 19 January 1939 Carrie Chapman Catt expresses a willingness to write in support of the book's publication, apparently in response to a request from Church Terrell, but notes, interestingly, that there is "difficulty getting feminist books published." Although most publishers commended the book, they all agreed it was too long and were worried about a market for it. Some were willing to publish the work if Church Terrell could supply a subvention to underwrite the first copies. Beverly Washington Jones, Church Terrell's biographer, reports that as a last resort Church Terrell turned to a vanity press, Ransdell Company, which issued one thousand copies. The book sold, but Church Terrell was unable to interest any publisher in a second edition (Jones, *Quest for Equality: The Life and Writings of Mary Eliza Church Terrell, 1863–1954* [Brooklyn: Carlson Publishing, 1990], 63).

Although only two reviews of the work are listed in the *Book Review Digest,* the book was reviewed in a number of small newspapers and journals throughout the country as well as the *Journal of Negro History* and the *Journal of Negro Education.* The *Digest* highlights her education at Oberlin and abroad, her work as a teacher, and her service on "committees of organizations working for the advancement of her race." The clippings file in the Mary Church Terrell papers at the Library of Congress has a number of reviews but none from the *New York Times, Washington Post,* or any other major metropolitan paper.

2. This quote, unidentified in the original, is apparently from Ralph J. Bunche. A copy of his comments without a date or source is included in the clippings file of the Church Terrell papers in a signed typescript. Bunche identifies himself as head of the Department of Political Science at Howard University. These comments may have been Bunche's response to Church Terrell's efforts to gain endorsements for her work to expedite its publication. Interestingly, the review in the *Journal of Negro Education* (X: 2, April 1941, 262–64) by Charles H. Wesley, a professor of history and dean of the Graduate School at Howard University, specifically refutes this claim, listing various other earlier published autobiographies by Black women.

3. No author, no title. *Christian Century* (30 October 1940): 1346.

4. H. G. Wells, "Preface," in Mary Church Terrell, *A Colored Woman in a White World* (Washington, D.C.: Ransdell, 1940). Subsequent references to this source will be cited as page numbers until otherwise indicated.

5. This is the title referred to in her correspondence with various publishers.

6. Jones, *Quest for Equality,* 71–86. This chapter contains two delightful pictures of Church Terrell, complete with hat and gloves, involved in picketing facilities.

7. The most condensed and vivid account of racial prejudice in Church Terrell's book is chapter 39, "The Colored Man's Paradise," which is a much more personalized narrative of the materials contained in her speech "What It Means to be Colored in the Capital of the United States" (1906); this speech is reprinted in Karlyn Kohrs

Campbell, *Man Cannot Speak For Her,* vol. 2 (New York: Praeger, 1989). Chapter 38, "Crossing the Color Line," explores that solution to the obstacles confronting Black Americans.

8. The lynching referred to in this section is that of Thomas Moss, a successful merchant in Memphis, who was lynched in part because his financial success upset local white merchants. Moss was also a friend of Ida Wells Barnett, and his death stimulated her antilynching campaign. His death is mentioned in Wells Barnett's 1893 speech, "Southern Horrors: Lynch Law in All Its Phases."

9. Church Terrell's description of her first efforts to cook a magnificent Thanksgiving dinner for her husband (122), in part to defeat notions of the slovenliness and ineptitude of college-educated women as homemakers, will certainly still generate sympathetic chuckles from many women today.

10. "First Presidential Address to the National Association of Colored Women," reprinted in Hine, 135.

11. "Dr. Terrell, 90, Dies; Fought for Equality," *Washington Post,* 25 July 1954, M16.

12. Quoted in Hine, 87. Hine cites this to "First Lady in Tribute to Mary Church Terrell" in the *Washington Post* of 25 July 1954. I was unable to find this article in that edition of the paper, although that is the edition that contained Church Terrell's obituary.

13. Sharon Harley, "Beyond the Classroom: The Organizational Lives of Black Female Educators in the District of Columbia, 1890–1930," *Journal of Negro Education* 5 (1982): 256.

14. Paula Giddings, *When and Where I Enter: The Impact of Black Women on Race and Sex in America* (New York: Macmillan, 1984).

15. Martin Luther King, "I Have a Dream" speech, 28 August 1963.

CHAPTER 7: WHEN AND WHERE I ENTER

1. I have borrowed the title for this chapter from Giddings's book on Black women in the United States: *When and Where I Enter.*

2. Kenneth Burke, *A Grammar of Motives* (Berkeley: University of California Press, 1969), xv.

3. Burke, *Grammar,* xv.

4. Burke, *Grammar,* 127–322.

5. Burke, *Grammar,* 128.

6. Burke, *Grammar,* 131.

7. Burke, *Grammar,* 171.

8. Burke, *Grammar,* 288.

9. Howarth, "Some Principles," 88–89.

10. Barbara Welter, *Dimity Convictions: The American Woman in the Nineteenth Century* (Athens: Ohio University Press, 1976). Clearly, many women, those studied here among them, did not embrace these limitations fully or willingly. And for some socio-economic and ethnic groups, the cult of true womanhood was simply not relevant. Still, these attributes were firmly associated with middle-class women, a group

to which Cady Stanton, Shaw, Willard, and Church Terrell belonged. More important, their target audience was largely made up of middle-class women with some leisure; these womanly virtues were quite pertinent to them.

11. "My Opinion of Men," in *Glimpses of Fifty Years,* 603–4.

12. Jelinek, *Tradition,* "Preface," xiii.

13. Lerner, *Creation,* 116.

14. Smith, *Poetics,* 7–8.

15. Church Terrell, *Colored Woman,* 426–27.

16. Gunn, *Autobiography,* 8.

17. Martha Solomon, *A Voice of Their Own: The Woman Suffrage Press, 1848–1910* (Tuscaloosa: University of Alabama Press, 1991).

18. "Some Principles," 86.

19. "Autobiography as Defacement," 930.

20. Shaw, *Story,* 337.

21. Willard, *Glimpses,* 695.

22. Patricia Spacks, "Selves in Hiding," 112.

23. Lerner, *Creation,* 12–13.

24. Lerner, *Creation,* 274.

25. Lerner, *Creation,* 13.

26. Lerner, *Creation,* 279.

27. Campbell, *Man Cannot,* vol. 1, 49.

28. Lorraine Code, *Rhetorical Spaces: Essays on Gendered Locations* (New York: Routledge, 1995), ix–x.

BIBLIOGRAPHY

Adams, Elmer C., and Warren Dunham Foster. *Heroines of Modern Progress*. New York: Macmillan, 1929.

Adams, Timothy Dow. *Telling Lies in Modern American Autobiography*. Chapel Hill: University of North Carolina Press, 1990.

Agar, Michael. "Stories, Background Knowledge and Themes: Problems in the Analysis of Life History Narrative." *American Ethnologist* 7 (May 1980): 223–39.

Andrews, William L. "The Changing Moral Discourse of Nineteenth-Century African American Women's Autobiography: Harriet Jacobs and Elizabeth Keckley." In *De/Colonizing the Subject: The Politics of Gender in Women's Autobiography*, edited by Sidonie Smith and Julia Watson, 225–41. Minneapolis: University of Minnesota Press, 1992.

———. "Introduction." In *African American Autobiography: A Collection of Critical Essays*, edited by William L. Andrews, 1–7. Englewood Cliffs, N.J.: Prentice-Hall, 1993.

———, ed. *African American Autobiography: A Collection of Critical Essays*. Englewood Cliffs, N.J.: Prentice-Hall, 1993.

Angrosino, Michael V. "Symbolic Leadership: An Interactive Analysis of Caribbean Political Autobiographies." *Biography* 15 (Summer 1992): 261–85.

Auerbach, Nina. *Woman and the Demon: The Life of a Victorian Myth*. Cambridge, Mass.: Harvard University Press, 1982.

Babcock, Bernie. *An Uncrowned Queen: The Story of the Life of Frances E. Willard Told for Young People*. Chicago: Fleming H. Revell Company, 1902.

Bakan, David. *The Duality of Human Existence: An Essay on Psychology and Religion*. Chicago: Rand McNally and Company, 1966.

Barros, Carolyn A. "Figura, Persona, Dynamis: Autobiography and Change." *Biography* 15 (Winter 1992): 1–28.

Bates, E. Stuart. *Inside Out: An Introduction to Autobiography*. New York: Sheridan House, 1937.

Benson, Thomas W. "Rhetoric and Autobiography: The Case of Malcolm X." *Quarterly Journal of Speech* 60 (February 1974): 1–13.

Benstock, Shari, ed. *The Private Self: Theory and Practice of Women's Autobiographical Writings*. Chapel Hill: University of North Carolina Press, 1988.

Blasing, Mutlu Konuk. *The Art of Life: Studies in American Autobiographical Literature*. Austin: University of Texas Press, 1977.

Bordin, Ruth. *Frances Willard: A Biography*. Chapel Hill: University of North Carolina Press, 1986.

———. *Woman and Temperance: The Quest for Power and Liberty, 1873–1900.* Philadelphia: Temple University Press, 1981.

Braxton, Joanne M. "Crusader for Justice: Ida B. Wells." In *African American Autobiography: A Collection of Critical Essays,* edited by William L. Andrews, 90–112. Englewood Cliffs, N.J.: Prentice-Hall, 1993.

Brown, Mary Ellen. "Personal Experience Stories, Autobiography, and Ideology." *Fabula: Journal of Folklore Studies* 31 (1990): 254–61.

Bruneau, Marie-Florine. "The Writing of History as Fiction and Ideology: The Case of Madame Guyon." *Feminist Issues* 5 (Spring 1985): 27–38.

Bruss, Elizabeth W. *Autobiographical Acts: The Changing Situation of a Literary Genre.* Baltimore: Johns Hopkins University Press, 1976.

Buechler, Steven M. *The Transformation of the Woman Suffrage Movement: The Case of Illinois, 1850–1920.* New Brunswick, N.J.: Rutgers University Press, 1986.

Campbell, Karlyn Kohrs. *Man Cannot Speak for Her: A Critical Study of Early Feminist Rhetoric.* New York: Praeger, 1989.

Caroli, Betty Boyd. "Women Speak Out for Reform." In *The Rhetoric of Protest and Reform: 1878–1898,* edited by Paul H. Boase, 212–31. Athens: Ohio University Press, 1980.

Clark, Arthur Melville. *Autobiography: Its Genesis and Phases.* Essex, U.K.: Oliver and Boyd, 1935.

Clay Bassard, Katherine. "Gender and Genre: Black Women's Autobiography and the Ideology of Literacy." *African American Review* 26 (1992): 119–29.

Collingwood, R. G. *An Autobiography.* Oxford: Oxford University Press, 1939.

Cooley, Thomas. *Educated Lives: The Rise of Modern Autobiography in America.* Columbus: Ohio State University Press, 1976.

Couser, G. Thomas. *Altered Egos: Authority in American Autobiography.* Oxford: Oxford University Press, 1989.

Cox, James. "Autobiography and America." *Virginia Quarterly Review* 47 (Spring 1971): 252–77.

Culley, Margo. "What a Piece of Work is 'Woman'! An Introduction." In *American Women's Autobiography: Fea(s)ts of Memory,* edited by Margo Culley, 3–31. Madison: University of Wisconsin Press, 1992.

———, ed. *American Women's Autobiography: Fea(s)ts of Memory.* Madison: University of Wisconsin Press, 1992.

Davies, Carole Boyce. "Collaboration and the Ordering Imperative in Life Story Production." In *De/Colonizing the Subject: The Politics of Gender in Women's Autobiography,* edited by Sidonie Smith and Julia Watson, 3–19. Minneapolis: University of Minnesota Press, 1992.

———. "Private Selves and Public Spaces: Autobiography and the African Woman Writer." *CLA Journal* 34 (March 1991): 267–89.

de Man, Paul. "Autobiography of De-facement." *MLN* 94 (December 1979): 919–30.

Denison Democrat, 12 February 1882, Scrapbook 15, p. 17. Willard Memorial Library, WCTU National Headquarters, Evanston, IL.

De Swarte Gifford, Carolyn. "Home Protection: The WCTU's Conversion to Woman Suffrage." In *Gender, Ideology, and Action: Historical Perspectives on Women's Public Lives,* edited by Janet Sharistanian, 95–120. New York: Greenwood Press, 1986.

Doherty, Thomas P. "American Autobiography and Ideology." In *The American Autobiography: A Collection of Critical Essays,* edited by Albert E. Stone, 95–108. Englewood Cliffs, N.J.: Prentice-Hall, 1981.

Dolan, Marc. "The (Hi)story of Their Lives: Mythic Autobiography and 'The Lost Generation.'" *Journal of American Studies* 27 (April 1993): 35–56.

Dow, Bonnie J. "Frances E. Willard (1839–1898), Reinventor of 'True Womanhood.'" In *Women Public Speakers in the United States, 1800–1925: A Bio-Critical Sourcebook,* edited by Karlyn Kohrs Campbell, 476–89. Westport, Conn.: Greenwood Press, 1993.

———. "The 'Womanhood' Rationale in the Woman Suffrage Rhetoric of Frances E. Willard." *Southern Communication Journal* 56 (Summer 1991): 298–307.

Duster, Alfreda M., ed. *Crusade for Justice: The Autobiography of Ida B. Wells.* Chicago: University of Chicago Press, 1970.

Eakin, Paul John. *Fictions in Autobiography: Studies in the Art of Self-Invention.* Princeton: Princeton University Press, 1985.

Earhart, Mary. *Frances Willard: From Prayers to Politics.* Chicago: University of Chicago Press, 1944.

Egan, Susanna. *Patterns of Experience in Autobiography.* Chapel Hill: University of North Carolina Press, 1984.

Egerton, George. "Politics and Autobiography: Political Memoir as Polygenre." *Biography* 15 (Summer 1992): 221–42.

Evanston Index, 26 October 1895, Scrapbook 70, p. 93. Willard Memorial Library, WCTU National Headquarters, Evanston, IL.

Fisher, Walter R. *Human Communication as Narration: Toward a Philosophy of Reason, Value, and Action.* Columbia: University of South Carolina Press, 1987.

Fleishman, Avrom. *Figures of Autobiography: The Language of Self-Writing in Victorian and Modern England.* Berkeley: University of California Press, 1983.

———. "Personal Myth: Three Victorian Autobiographers." In *Approaches to Victorian Autobiography,* edited by George P. Landow, 215–34. Athens: Ohio University Press, 1979.

Gilbert, Sandra M., and Susan Gubar. "Sexual Linguistics: Gender, Language, Sexuality." *New Literary History* 16 (Spring 1985): 515–43.

Gilead, Sarah. "Emigrant Selves: Narrative Stories in Three Women's Autobiographies." *Criticism* 30 (Winter 1988): 43–62.

Goldman, Emma. *Living My Life*. Reprint. Salt Lake City, Utah: Gibbs M. Smith, 1982.

Goldman, Janice G. "Discourse Autobiography as a Path to Feminist Consciousness." *Journal of Feminist Family Therapy* 4 (1992): 69–78.

Gordon, Anna Adams. *The Beautiful Life of Frances E. Willard (A Memorial Volume)*. Chicago: WCTU Press, 1898.

———. *The Life of Frances E. Willard*. Evanston, Ill.: WCTU Press, 1921.

———, ed. *What Frances E. Willard Said*. Evanston, Ill.: WCTU Press, 1905.

Grele, Ronald J. "Movement without Aim: Methodological and Theoretical Problems in Oral History." In *Envelopes of Sound: Six Practitioners Discuss the Method, Theory and Practice of Oral History and Oral Testimony,* edited by Ronald J. Grele, 126–54. Chicago: Precedent Publishing, 1975.

Griffin, Charles J. G. "The Rhetoric of Form in Conversion Narratives." *Quarterly Journal of Speech* 76 (May 1990): 152–63.

Gunn, Janet Varner. *Autobiography: Toward a Poetics of Experience*. Philadelphia: University of Pennsylvania Press, 1982.

Gusdorf, Georges. "Conditions and Limits of Autobiography." In *Autobiography: Essays Theoretical and Critical,* edited by James Olney, 28–48. Princeton: Princeton University Press, 1980.

Gusfield, Joseph R. "Status Conflicts and the Changing Ideologies of the American Temperance Movement." In *Society, Culture, and Drinking Patterns,* edited by David J. Pittman and Charles R. Snyder, 101–20. Carbondale: Southern Illinois University Press, 1962.

———. *Symbolic Crusade: Status Politics and the American Temperance Movement*. 2nd ed. Urbana: University of Illinois Press, 1986.

Halpern, Ben. "'Myth' and 'Ideology' in Modern Usage." *History and Theory* 1 (1961): 129–49.

Hart, Francis R. "Notes for an Anatomy of Modern Autobiography." *New Literary History* 1 (Spring 1970): 485–511.

Hodges, John O. "The Divided Self and the Quest for Wholeness in Black American Autobiography." *Soundings* 73 (Summer/Fall 1990): 423–42.

Howarth, William L. "Some Principles of Autobiography." In *Autobiography: Essays Theoretical and Critical,* edited by James Olney, 84–114. Princeton: Princeton University Press, 1980.

Howells, William Dean. "Editor's Easy Chair." *Harper's Monthly Magazine* (October 1909): 795–98.

JanMohamed, Abdul R. "Negating the Negation as a Form of Affirmation in Minority Discourse: The Construction of Richard Wright as Subject." *Cultural Critique* 7 (Fall 1989): 245–66.

Jay, Paul. *Being in the Text: Self-Representation from Wordsworth to Roland Barthes*. Ithaca: Cornell University Press, 1984.

Jehlen, Myra. "Archimedes and the Paradox of Feminist Criticism." *Signs: Journal of Women in Culture and Society* 6 (Summer 1981): 575–601.

Jelinek, Estelle C. *The Tradition of Women's Autobiography: From Antiquity to the Present*. Boston: Twayne, 1986.

———, ed. *Women's Autobiography: Essays in Criticism*. Bloomington: Indiana University Press, 1980.

Jimerson, Randall C., Francis X. Blouin, and Charles A. Isetts, eds. *Guide to the Microfilm Edition of Temperance and Prohibition Papers*. Ann Arbor, University of Michigan, 1977.

Judson, Clara Ingram. *Pioneer Girl: The Early Life of Frances Willard*. New York: Rand McNally and Company, 1939.

Kaplan, Andrew. "The Rhetoric of Circumstance in Autobiography." *Rhetorica* 10 (Winter 1992): 71–98.

Kolodny, Annette. "A Map for Rereading: Or, Gender and the Interpretation of Literary Texts." *New Literary History* 11 (Spring 1980): 451–67.

———. "The Lady's Not for Spurning: Kate Millett and the Critics." In *Women's Autobiography: Essays in Criticism,* edited by Estelle C. Jelinek, 238–59. Bloomington: Indiana University Press, 1980.

Kramarae, Cheris. *Women and Men Speaking: Frameworks for Analysis*. Rowley, Mass.: Newbury House Publishers, 1981.

Leeman, Richard W. *"Do Everything Reform": The Oratory of Frances E. Willard*. New York: Greenwood Press, 1992.

Lejeune, Philippe. *On Autobiography*. Translated by Katnerine Leary. Edited by Paul John Eakin. Minneapolis: University of Minnesota Press, 1989.

Lionnet, Françoise. *Autobiographical Voices: Race, Gender, Self-Portraiture*. Ithaca: Cornell University Press, 1989.

Lloyd, David. "Genet's Genealogy: European Minorities and the Ends of the Canon." *Cultural Critique* 6 (Spring 1987): 161–85.

Lutz, Alma. *Created Equal: A Biography of Elizabeth Cady Stanton*. New York: John Day Company, 1940.

MacKethan, Lucinda H. "Mother Wit: Humor in Afro-American Women's Autobiography." *Studies in American Humor* 4 (Spring/Summer 1985): 51–61.

Mandel, Barrett John. "The Autobiographer's Art." *Journal of Aesthetics and Art Criticism* 27 (Winter 1968): 215–26.

———. "Autobiography Reflection Trained on Mystery." *Prairie Schooner* 46 (Winter 1972/1973): 323–38.

———. "Full of Life Now." In *Autobiography: Essays Theoretical and Critical,* edited by James Olney, 49–72. Princeton: Princeton University Press, 1980.

Marilley, Suzanne M. "Frances Willard and the Feminism of Fear." *Feminist Studies* 19 (Spring 1993): 123–46.

Mason, Mary G. "The Other Voice: Autobiographies of Women Writers." In *Autobiography: Essays Theoretical and Critical,* edited by James Olney, 207–35. Princeton: Princeton University Press, 1980.

McDowell, Deborah E. "In the First Place: Making Frederick Douglass and the Afro-American Narrative Tradition." In *African American Autobiography: A Collection of Critical Essays,* edited by William L. Andrews, 36–58. Englewood Cliffs, N.J.: Prentice-Hall, 1993.

Miller, Ida Tetreault. "Frances Elizabeth Willard: Religious Leader and Social Reformer." Ph.D. dissertation, Boston University, 1978.

Minutes of the National Woman's Christian Temperance Union. Chicago: WCTU Press, 1888.

"Miss Willard's Outburst." N.p., Scrapbook 70, p. 92. Willard Memorial Library, WCTU National Headquarters, Evanston, IL.

Morgan, David. "Masculinity, Autobiography and History." *Gender & History* 2 (Spring 1990): 34–39.

Morris, John N. *Versions of the Self: Studies in English Autobiography from John Bunyan to John Stuart Mill.* New York: Basic Books, 1966.

Neuman, Shirley. "Autobiography and Questions of Gender: An Introduction." *Prose Studies* 14 (September 1991): 1–11.

Ochiai, Akiko. "Ida B. Wells and Her Crusade for Justice: An African American Woman's Testimonial Autobiography." *Soundings* 75 (Summer/Fall 1992): 365–81.

Oliver, Robert T. "Denouncing Demon Drink: Frances E. Willard and John B. Gough." In *History of Public Speaking in America.* Boston: Allyn and Bacon, 1965.

Olney, James. "Autobiography and the Cultural Moment: A Thematic, Historical, and Bibliographical Introduction." In *Autobiography: Essays Theoretical and Critical,* edited by Olney, 3–27. Princeton: Princeton University Press, 1980.

———. "The Autobiography of America" (review of *Altered Egos: Authority in American Autobiography* by G. Thomas Courser, *Recovering Literature's Lost Ground: Essays in American Autobiography* by James M. Cox, *The Complex Image: Faith and Method in American Autobiography* by Joseph Fichtelberg, and *Fabricating Lives: Explorations in American Autobiography* by Herbert Leibowitz). *American Literary History* 3 (Summer 1991): 376–95.

———. *Metaphors of Self: The Meaning of Autobiography.* Princeton: Princeton University Press, 1972.

———, ed. *Autobiography: Essays Theoretical and Critical.* Princeton: Princeton University Press, 1980.

Oravec, Christine. "The Ideological Significance of Discursive Form: A Response to Solomon and Perkins." *Communication Studies* 42 (Winter 1991): 383–91.

Oxford English Dictionary. 2nd ed. Oxford: Clarendon Press, 1989.

Pascal, Roy. *Design and Truth in Autobiography.* Cambridge, Mass.: Harvard University Press, 1960.

Personal Narratives Group, ed. *Interpreting Women's Lives: Feminist Theory and Personal Narratives*. Bloomington: Indiana University Press, 1989.

Pilling, John. *Autobiography and Imagination: Studies in Self-Scrutiny*. London: Routledge & Kegan Paul, 1981.

Renza, Louis A. "The Veto of the Imagination: A Theory of Autobiography." In *Autobiography: Essays Theoretical and Critical,* edited by James Olney, 268–95. Princeton: Princeton University Press, 1980.

Review of *My Happy Half Century* by Frances E. Willard. *Glasgow Herald,* 11 January 1895, Scrapbook 35, p. 18. Willard Memorial Library, WCTU National Headquarters, Evanston, IL.

———. *Guardian,* 9 January 1895, Scrapbook 35, p. 17. Willard Memorial Library, WCTU National Headquarters, Evanston, IL.

———. *London Weekly Sun,* 13 January 1895, Scrapbook 35, p. 19. Willard Memorial Library, WCTU National Headquarters, Evanston, IL.

———. N.p., 29 December 1894, Scrapbook 35, p. 14. Willard Memorial Library, WCTU National Headquarters, Evanston, IL.

———. N.p., n.d., Scrapbook 35, p. 23. Willard Memorial Library, WCTU National Headquarters, Evanston, IL.

———. *Queen,* 9 February 1895, Scrapbook 35, p. 21. Willard Memorial Library, WCTU National Headquarters, Evanston, IL.

Sayre, Robert F. *The Examined Self: Benjamin Franklin, Henry Adams, Henry James*. Princeton: Princeton University Press, 1964.

Shaw, Anna Howard. With Elizabeth Jordan. *The Story of a Pioneer*. New York: Harper and Bros., 1915.

Showalter, Elaine. "Feminist Criticism in the Wilderness." In *Writing and Sexual Difference,* edited by Elizabeth Abel, 9–35. Chicago: University of Chicago Press, 1982.

Slagell, Amy Rose. "A Good Woman Speaking Well: The Oratory of Frances E. Willard." Ph.D. dissertation, University of Wisconsin—Madison, 1992.

Smith, Sidonie. "The Autobiographical Manifesto: Identities, Temporalities, Politics." *Prose Studies* 14 (September 1991): 186–212.

———. "Construing Truths in Lying Mouths: Truthtelling in Women's Autobiography." *Studies in the Literary Imagination* 23 (Fall 1990): 145–63.

———. *A Poetics of Women's Autobiography: Marginality and the Fictions of Self-Representation*. Bloomington: Indiana University Press, 1987.

———. "Self, Subject, and Resistance: Marginalities and Twentieth-Century Autobiographical Practice." *Tulsa Studies in Women's Literature* 9 (Spring 1990): 11–24.

———. "Who's Talking/Who's Talking Back? The Subject of Personal Narrative." *Signs: Journal of Women in Culture and Society* 18 (Winter 1993): 392–407.

Smith, Sidonie, and Julia Watson, eds. *De/Colonizing the Subject: The Politics of Gender in Women's Autobiography*. Minneapolis: University of Minnesota Press, 1992.

Solomon, Martha. "Autobiographies as Rhetorical Narratives: Elizabeth Cady Stanton and Anna Howard Shaw as 'New Women.'" *Communication Studies* 42 (Winter 1991): 354–70.

Somerset, Lady Henry. "White and Black in America: An Interview with Miss Willard." *Westminster Gazette* [May 1894], Scrapbook 69, p. 20. Willard Memorial Library, WCTU National Headquarters, Evanston, IL.

Spacks, Patricia Meyer. "Reflecting Women." *Yale Review* 63 (October 1973): 26–42.

———. "Selves in Hiding." In *Women's Autobiography: Essays in Criticism,* edited by Estelle C. Jelinek, 112–32. Bloomington: Indiana University Press, 1980.

———. "Stages of Self: Notes on Autobiography and the Life Cycle." In *The American Autobiography: A Collection of Critical Essays,* edited by Albert E. Stone, 44–60. Englewood Cliffs, N.J.: Prentice-Hall, 1981.

———. "Women's Stories, Women's Selves." *Hudson Review* 30 (Spring 1977): 29–46.

Spengemann, William C. *The Forms of Autobiography: Episodes in the History of Literary Genre.* New Haven: Yale University Press, 1980.

Spengemann, William C., and L. R. Lundquist. "Autobiography and the American Myth." *American Quarterly* 17 (Fall 1965): 501–19.

Sprinker, Michael. "Fictions of the Self: The End of Autobiography." In *Autobiography: Essays Theoretical and Critical,* edited by James Olney, 321–42. Princeton: Princeton University Press, 1980.

Stanton, Domna C., ed. *The Female Autograph: Theory and Practice of Autobiography from the Tenth to the Twentieth Century.* Chicago: University of Chicago Press, 1984.

Stanton, Elizabeth Cady. *Eighty Years and More: Reminiscences 1815–1897.* New York: Schocken Books, 1971.

Starobinski, Jean. "The Style of Autobiography." In *Autobiography: Essays Theoretical and Critical,* edited by James Olney, 73–83. Princeton: Princeton University Press, 1980.

Stead, W. T. "The Uncrowned Queen of American Democracy." *Review of Reviews* 6 (November 1892): 427–44.

Steele, Peter. *The Autobiographical Passion: Studies in the Self on Show.* Melbourne: Melbourne University Press, 1989.

Stewart, Jane A. *The Frances Willard Book.* Philadelphia: Current Syndicate Co., 1906.

Stone, Albert E. *Autobiographical Occasions and Original Acts: Versions of American Identity from Henry Adams to Nate Shaw.* Philadelphia: University of Pennsylvania Press, 1982.

———, ed. *The American Autobiography: A Collection of Critical Essays.* Englewood Cliffs, N.J.: Prentice-Hall, 1981.

Strachey, Ray. *Frances Willard: Her Life and Work.* London: T. Fisher Unwin, 1912.

Strull, Heidi I. *The Evolution of the Autobiography from 1770–1850: A Comparative Study and Analysis.* New York: Peter Lang, 1985.

Susman, Warren I. "History and the American Intellectual: Uses of a Usable Past." *American Quarterly* 16 (Summer 1964): 243–63.

Taylor, Gordon O. *Studies in Modern American Autobiography*. London: Macmillan Press, 1983.

Thomas, Henry, and Dana Lee Thomas. *Living Biographies of Famous Women*. Garden City, N.Y.: Garden City Publishing Co., 1942.

Townsend, Harriet A. *Reminiscences of Famous Women*. New York: Evans-Penfold Company, 1916.

Trowbridge, Lydia Jones. *Frances Willard of Evanston*. Chicago: Willet, Clark & Company, 1938.

Watson, Julia, and Sidonie Smith. "De/Colonization and the Politics of Discourse in Women's Autobiographical Practices." In *De/Colonizing the Subject: The Politics of Gender in Women's Autobiography,* edited by Smith and Watson, xiii–xxxi. Minneapolis: University of Minnesota Press, 1992.

Weintraub, Karl J. "Autobiography and Historical Consciousness." *Critical Inquiry* 1 (June 1975): 821–48.

——— . *The Value of the Individual: Self and Circumstance in Autobiography*. Chicago: University of Chicago Press, 1978.

Weixlmann, Joe. "African American Autobiography in the Twentieth Century: A Bibliographical Essay." *Black American Literature Forum* 24 (Summer 1990): 375–415.

Welter, Barbara. "The Cult of True Womanhood." *American Quarterly* 18 (1966): 151–74.

Wethered, H. N. *The Curious Art of Autobiography: From Benvenuto Cellini to Rudyard Kipling*. New York: Philosophical Library, 1956.

Whiting, Lilian. *Women Who Have Ennobled Life*. Philadelphia: Union Press, 1915.

Willard, Frances E. *Glimpses of Fifty Years: The Autobiography of an American Woman*. Boston: George M. Smith & Co., 1889.

——— . *My Happy Half-Century: The Autobiography of an American Woman*. Edited by Frances E. Cook. London: Ward, Lock & Co., [1894].

Witt, Florence. *Frances E. Willard: The Story of a Noble Woman*. London: Sunday School Union, [1898].

INDEX